★

raising reds

L CUMMINGS.

RAISING REDS

The Young Pioneers,

Radical Summer Camps,

and Communist Political Culture

in the United States

Paul C. Mishler

columbia university press

new york

COLUMBIA UNIVERSITY PRESS

Publishers Since 1893
New York   Chichester, West Sussex
Copyright © 1999 by Columbia University Press

Library of Congress Cataloging-in-Publication Data
Mishler, Paul C.   Raising reds : the young pioneers, radical summer camps, and communist
political culture in the United States / Paul C. Mishler.
    p. cm.
    Includes bibliographical references and index.
    ISBN 0–231–11044–8 (cloth : alk. paper). — ISBN 0–231–11045–6 (pbk. : alk. paper).
    1. Communist Party of the United States. Young Pioneers—History.
2. Communism and youth—United States—History.   3. Children—United States—
Social conditions.   4. Children and politics—United States—History.   5. Communist
education—United States—History.
I. Title.
HX81.M57   1999
324.273'75'09—dc21   98–39593

∞

Casebound editions of Columbia University Press books are printed on permanent and durable
acid-free paper.
Printed in the United States of America
c 10 9 8 7 6 5 4 3 2 1
p 10 9 8 7 6 5 4 3 2

For
ELLIOT G. MISHLER

And in memory of
ANITA L. MISHLER

"You have sown the seeds of freedom in your daughters and your sons."
–TOMMY SANDS

contents

acknowledgments

The friendship, knowledge, and experience of many friends and colleagues enriched my life during the writing of this book.

My deepest appreciation goes to those men and women who participated in the activities described here. In the course of my research I spoke with scores of former campers and organizers of left-wing children's activities. Their insight was invaluable. I have used their stories to fashion one of my own. Writing about their lives and analyzing their activities deepened the respect I feel for these people.

I would especially like to thank Elsie Suller, the long-time director of Camp Kinderland; Edith Segal; Courtney Cazden; Joan Studer Levine; and Ann Filardo. Ernest Rymer, in particular, spoke with me extensively, contributing insight and wit based on his long experience in the activities that are the subject of this book. He provided me with otherwise unobtainable papers and pamphlets. Without his support early on I would never have been able to complete this project. Unfortunately, Ernest died in the summer of 1985 before this work could be completed.

Librarians at the Catherwood Library at Cornell University, the New York State University at Albany, the Tamiment Institute at New York University, the Reference Center for Marxist Studies in New York, the YIVO Institute for Jewish Research, and the library of the Center for Puerto Rican Studies at Hunter College, New York, all helped me identify and track down essential materials. Dottie Rubin at International Publishers opened the doors to the International Publishers archives, where I found many of the children's books discussed in chapter 6.

Harry Stoneback of SUNY, New Paltz, gave me access to the Norman Studer Papers and the photgraphic archives of Camp Woodland. Shari Segel and Paul Goldberg allowed me to use their personal collection of photographs of Edith Segal, and Marvin and Florence Itzkowitz provided me with the photographs of Camp Kinderland.

I have enjoyed the support and encouragement of many people, especially Gregory Kaster, Kate Wittenstein, John Beck, Bill Askins, and Rachel Kranz. Rachel edited an earlier version of this manuscript.

Portions of this book have been presented as conference papers, and Kenneth Teitelbaum, Milton Cantor, and Gerald Zahavi provided appreciated criticism and commentary. I have had the pleasure of discussing the history of Communism in the United States with Roger Keeran, Dorothy Fennell, Judy Kaplan, Norman Markowitz, Linn Shapiro, Kate Weigand, Van Gosse, and Robin Kelley, and our shared interests and commitments go far beyond the scope of this book. Robin Kelley, in particular, has been a great supporter of my work. Judy Kaplan and Linn Shapiro have been working on the Red Diaper Baby experience, and talking with them has been invaluable. Thanks to all of you. I also want to thank Ann Miller, my editor at Columbia University Press. The anonymous reviewers who read this in manuscript for Columbia University Press provided many useful comments and suggestions.

My family has shared the commitments that give purpose to this book. With Gerrie Casey I have shared a life of intellectual and political passion. She has cast an affectionate and critical eye on all my writing and has shared with me the work of building a family of my own. The birth of our son Max transformed me from a radical student into a radical parent, and his growing up continues to give me insight into the concerns of the radical parents of the past. Finally, this book is dedicated to my own parents, Elliot and Anita Mishler. As intellectuals and radicals they supported this project and have inspired me in my life. They taught my brother Mark and me that the world is out there to be changed.

★

raising reds

introduction

Tanya Rosenberg grew up in the Allerton Avenue "Coops," a Bronx cooperative apartment complex built by Communists during the 1920s. She described the festive atmosphere of May Day there during the 1920s or early 1930s:

> When you opened the door and walked into the court, you would think it was a world holiday. All our children were out early in the court, dressed beautifully, waiting for the time to leave and join the demonstration. Such excitement! I can say that was the only holiday when you really felt a holiday spirit, all through the halls and courts.[1]

Many of the children in the "Coops" belonged to the Young Pioneers of America, the children's organization of the Communist Party. The Young Pioneers in the Bronx staged sit-ins to integrate recreation facilities, propagandized against the Boy Scouts, campaigned against militarist curricula and for fair disciplinary procedures in schools, and stayed out of school to march with their parents on May Day. The Bronx Pioneers were part of an effort made by Communist Party members to create institutions that would transmit their political values and beliefs to children. The Communist Children's Movement, as it was called, included, along with the Pioneers, after-school programs; summer camps; and the "junior" sections of Communist-led organizations such as the International Workers Order, the League of Struggle for Negro

Rights, the International Labor Defense, and children's organizations created during Communist-led strikes of miners and textile workers.

Between the 1920s and the 1950s, the children's programs of the Communist movement were an important factor in the development of a Communist political culture in the United States. Because the socialization of children into the values, beliefs, and mores of the adults of their community is such an important part of any culture, the examination of the children's activities of the Communist Party is a window into that political culture. Compared with Communist efforts to organize trade unions or their campaigns to free Tom Moony or the Scottsboro defendants, the children's organizations played a small role in the overall political strategy of the Communist Party, but the children's activities did help build spirit and cohesion within the Communist movement. Furthermore, these activities helped make the Communist Party in the United States a movement of families. Most Communist parties elsewhere were primarily male organizations, and even the families of militants were often outside the party.[2]

Foremost in my concern is understanding the Communist Party's efforts to develop a political culture in which the Marxist analysis of politics and economics was elaborated into a way of life. I am not, therefore, concerned with the success or failure of their efforts in transmitting their values and beliefs to their children, or with the effect of these programs on the political, personal, or psychological development of the children. This is not because the children's perspective—or rather, *adult* memory of childhood experience filtered through time—is unimportant. Rather, I want to look at these activities for what they illustrate about the culture of the adults who created them.

The political culture of the Communist movement and the politics of the Communist Party were mutually informing. Communist politics during the period covered in this study—from the early years of the Communist Party during the 1920s through the 1950s—was based on the party's self-identification as a Marxist-Leninist organization committed to bringing about a socialist revolution in the United States. Its policies were oriented to advancing this political goal. Communists believed that the Communist Party of the Soviet Union was at the center of an international movement with a common perspective and common strategy. At the same time, they tried to apply the positions and policies adopted by the international Communist movement to the social and political struggles in the United States.

The relationship between the Communist Party of the United States and that of the Soviet Union is the subject of much of the debate on the history of the American Communist Party. Writers such as Theodore Draper, and more recently Harvey Klehr and John Haynes, maintain that the CP in the United States followed directions from the CPSU, and can only be understood as an institution whose aims and policies were defined by the Soviet government. Historians such as Maurice Isserman, Robin Kelley, and Mark Naison, who for the most part are sympathetic with the Communists' critique of American society, even while disagreeing with many of its policies, have looked at the Communist Party as an expression of a native radical tradition defined as much by its activities in the United States as by its relationship with the Soviet Union.[3]

In this study, I am influenced by these latter historians. The activities for children organized by U.S. Communists were neither central to American Communists' political interests nor important to the Soviet Union. At the same time, U.S. Communists identified strongly with the Soviet Union, and their idea of what the Soviet Union was like influenced their political perspective and the political culture that developed among them.

The political culture that grew up in the institutional context of the political activities of the Communist Party reflected the ways that identification with the Communist movement became a way of life for American Communists. Within the culture were issues that Communists faced that were not expressed as clearly as the political programs and strategies of the party itself. In the Communist political culture, activists and sympathizers, militants and their families, confronted the dual dilemma of what it meant to be a revolutionary and what it meant to be an American. These issues formed the cultural/ideological matrix in which they organized activities designed to acculturate their children.

The dilemmas and paradoxes involved in being both American and revolutionary has particular resonance for American Communists. Communists were often immigrants or the children of immigrants, and like many of their nonradical compatriots were ambivalent about the transitions to becoming American that took place during this period.

All immigrants to the United States during the late nineteenth and early twentieth centuries confronted the differences between their own culture and that of their new home. This was often a stressful and painful experience for them, as has been amply documented by historians of immigration. For nonradical immigrants, the promises of American life could compensate for the terrible living conditions they endured, and for their alienation from the dominant culture. For radical immigrants, this process was made more complicated by their critical political stance toward American society. Radicals viewed the promise of America as empty or contradictory. Their hostility toward American culture was manifested in the tenaciousness with which radical immigrants held onto their ethnic cultures, clustering in radical enclaves in immigrant communities, often organized around the radical foreign-language press.

The official position of the Communist movement in the United States was, at least initially, to discourage the maintenance of ethnic distinctions. Indeed, the Americanization of the immigrant radicals had been seen by Marxist theoreticians since the nineteenth century as the way in which Marxist ideas could be brought to the American working class. The differences between Marxist theoreticians and the base of the socialist movement was evident early in the history of American socialism. Friedrich Engels himself criticized the ethnic isolation of the German-American socialists, which he saw as an impediment to the development of the socialist movement in the United States:

> This party [the predominantly German-American Socialist Labor Party] is called upon to play a very important part in the movement. But in order to do so they will have to doff every remnant of their foreign garb. They will have to become out and out American. They cannot expect the Americans to come to them; they, the minority and the immigrants, must go to the Americans who are the vast majority and the natives.[4]

American Communists shared Engels's view and looked to the gradual Americanization of radical immigrants, and particularly their children, as a means of expanding the influence of their movement. This goal was contradictory. They understood that Americanization was going to occur regardless of the wishes of the immigrants. Furthermore, the political importance that the Communist Party came to ascribe to African Americans was predicated on the view that in the future the crucial ethnic divisions in American life would be those based on skin color, not on European countries of ancestry. The myopia of the Communists was that they thought that the incorporation of radical immigrants into American culture would lead to greater radicalization among nonimmigrant workers. In fact, as the bonds of ethnic allegiance among radical immigrants weakened, their radical politics weakened too.

Because of their negative view of ethnicity, Communists' political strategy was at first directed toward breaking out of the confines of the enclaves of radical immigrants where much of the Communist Party's strength was located. Communists attempted to dissolve the radical ethnic organizations and incorporate their membership into an "American" Communist Party. Accordingly, between 1925 and 1928, as part of the "Bolshevization" of the Communist Party, the foreign-language federations of the CP were disbanded. These federations were creations of the Socialist Party, and they had been crucial in the founding of the Communist Party. The Slavic federations in particular had participated in the founding of the Communist Party and had switched their affiliation from the Socialists to the Communist Party as a bloc.

After 1928, party membership became increasingly the province of English-speaking radicals. In part, this was because of the decrease in immigration after the passage of the Immigration Restriction Act of 1924, but it was also because many members of the foreign-language federations did not keep up their membership in the Communist Party itself; instead, they joined the Communist-led fraternal societies, many of which joined together in 1930 to form the International Workers Order. The IWO was a federation of mutual-benefit societies organized along ethnic lines. In addition to providing low-cost insurance to its members, its constituent organizations maintained ethnic radical culture through their sponsorship of singing groups, folkdance ensembles, and children's activities.

By the 1930s, the English-speaking children of immigrants were changing the composition of the Communist Party. Some of these new activists had been brought up within the Communist movement of the 1920s; others came to the Communist Party out of the struggles led by the party during the depression. For this new generation of American-born Communists, the decision of whether to identify with American culture or with ethnic culture was more of a choice than it had been for their foreign-born parents. The IWO continued to grow throughout the 1930s even among this generation. Radicalism defined by ethnicity strongly attracted even the children of immigrants. Indeed, during the 1930s the membership of the IWO, which was always much greater than actual party membership, was among the most important bases of support for Communist political efforts. This was recognized by the Communist Party after 1936, when the Communist view of ethnicity came to resemble that of the IWO. The children's program of the IWO, which is the subject of chapter 4, was the major arena for Communist efforts among children during the 1930s.

Although the Communist Party had hoped that the Americanization of immigrant radicals would help it make inroads among "American" workers, it also sought to expand from its immigrant base by sponsoring organizing drives in areas and industries dominated by "American" workers. Its two most successful efforts in this regard, prior to participation in the Congress of Industrial Organizations (CIO) organizing drives of the mid-1930s, were the Gastonia, North Carolina, textile strike of 1929 and the organization of the National Miners Union, which developed in the late 1920s and the early 1930s out of a reform effort within the United Mine Workers union. In both cases the workers involved were predominantly native-born rather than immigrant.[5] In the organizing at Gastonia and in the mining communities, special organizers were sent by the Young Pioneers of America to organize children's sections of the unions. Stories about Gastonia and the National Miners Union were published in the *Young Pioneer* magazine and in the children's books published by the Communist Party during this period.

Out of their Gastonia and National Miners Union organizing drives came the special political-cultural relationship between folksong and the Communist movement. In North Carolina and in the Appalachian coal fields, New York Communists were first exposed to traditional Southern folksinging and saw how it could be used for political purposes in the singing of strikers and strike supporters from these communities. When Ella Mae Wiggins, a young striker and songwriter from Gastonia, was killed by police, her songs were published in the *Daily Worker* and the *New Masses*.[6] Among the singer-songwriters to come out of the efforts of the National Miners union were Florence Reece, author of the labor-movement classic "Which Side Are You On?"[7] and the family group of

Aunt Molly Jackson, her brother Jim Garland, and her half sister Sarah Ogun Gunning. Aunt Molly Jackson's song "Poor Miner's Farewell" was one of the first in the American folk idiom to be published in the *Red Song Book*, which was issued by the Workers Music League in 1932.[8] Jim Garland last recorded his best-known song, "The Death of Harry Simms"—about a young Young Communist League (YCL) organizer killed in Harlan County, Kentucky—at the Newport Folk Festival in 1963, bringing it to an entirely new generation.[9]

Indeed, folk songs became one of the most important mediums through which Communists connected their world to the traditions and culture of the United States. Singers such as Woody Guthrie, Leadbelly, Josh White, and Pete Seeger, who eventually helped to spark the folksong revival of the 1960s, reached their first audiences in the radical labor movement influenced by the Communist Party during the 1930s and 1940s.[10]

The paradigm within which American Communists played out the tension between "ethnic" and "American" history was that of the Marxist analysis of history. Marxism is both universal and particularist, descriptive and prescriptive. In its universal and descriptive form it is an explanation of human history as a whole. Because Marxism is concerned with transformations in modes of production and changes in grand historical epochs, it transcends national history. For people between nations, such as the immigrants to the United States, this aspect of Marxism could be particularly attractive.

If the struggle to define their place within an ethnic or national context provided one pole around which the children's activities of American Communism was organized, their revolutionary aspirations supplied the other. These revolutionary beliefs were a manifestation of utopian currents within Communist political culture. These currents included a complex mixture of European anarchist and socialist traditions, American utopian communalist traditions, the idealization of the Soviet Union, and, by the late 1930s, a view of American democracy itself.

Marxist movements, including the Communists, disavowed explicit utopianism. Basing themselves on Engels's critique of nineteenth-century utopian socialist theorists, Marxists counterpoised their own "scientific" or political socialism to the socialism of literature or desire. Socialists drew on Frederick Engels's *Socialism: Utopian and Scientific* to mark out the distinction between Marxism and earlier radicalisms in which the utopian element was more pronounced. Yet Engels's work was not an attack on utopianism per se. Rather, it was a critique of the forms that utopianism took in the era of early capitalism. Engels attacked utopias based on will and hope, rather than on political engagement and struggle. Indeed, Engels concluded his essay with a look toward the future, grounded in "history" but just as utopian as the visions he had derided earlier in his essay:

> With the seizing of the means of production . . . for the first time, man, in a certain sense, is finally marked off from the rest of the animal kingdom, and emerges from the mere animal conditions of existence into really human ones. . . . It is the ascent of man from the kingdom of necessity to the kingdom of freedom.[11]

The perspective of this study is that a form of utopianism is intrinsic to any radical project. It is the utopian or millennial vision that gives strength to the political and economic critique of society that is advanced by radicals. More than any particular campaign for civic justice or economic betterment, the hope that the world itself can be totally transformed is what distinguishes radicals from reformers. Eric Hobsbawm, the historian who has looked at this issue most extensively, has said that the millennial spirit "is present, almost by definition, in all revolutionary movements of whatever kind."[12]

In Marxist socialist movements, the radical utopian vision became masked. Marxists looked to history to justify their critique of capitalism, not to the future. The utopian vision remained, nonetheless. Marxist philosopher Ernst Bloch identified this as the "warm current" within Marxism. This warm current is the part of the socialist project that "transports human subjectivity into an imagined realm of freedom."[13]

The importance of this "warm current" within Marxism accounts for the continuing popularity among nineteenth-century socialists of books such as Bebel's *Women under Socialism,* Edward Bellamy's *Looking Backward,* and William Morris's *News from Nowhere.* Furthermore, in the United States the utopian aspect of nineteenth-century social criticism remained strong among Marxists. The extreme left of the socialist movement, many of whose adherents would become Communists after the Russian Revolution, were suspicious of reform and kept their focus on revolutionary transformation. At the same time, the availability of land and the relative openness of American society led Marxists to organize their own experimental communities, attempting to bring the world of the future closer through cooperative living and labor.[14]

Prior to the twentieth century, the utopian aspect was explicit in almost all political radicalism movements in the United States. Experiments in utopian living existed on the fringes of almost all of the reform or radical movements of the nineteenth century and activists in the more politically engaged movements often visited and were sympathetic to these experiments. It was not until the twentieth century that Marxism, or Marxist-inspired ideas, became dominant in American radicalism. With Marxism, American radicals absorbed the anti-utopianism that was characteristic of the mainstream Marxist tradition, particularly as it was interpreted by the leaders of German Social-Democracy, the guardians of Marxist orthodoxy within the Second International.

After the First World War, experiments in practical utopianism shifted from communities that emphasized common labor and ownership of property toward those in which the utopian expressions were in education and leisure. Communities grew up around radical adult-education institutions such as Commonwealth College in Mena, Arkansas[15] (itself a child of the Newllano Colony) and the anarchist Ferrer Modern School in New Jersey; during the 1920s and 1930s, Communists were involved with both. Thus, while "utopianism" continued to be a term of opprobrium for Marxists, there remained an undercurrent of sympathy for the utopian spirit, even among orthodox Communists. Mike Gold, the American Communist writer and literary critic, spent a summer at the Stelton Colony attached to the Ferrer Modern School in New Jersey. In a 1921 article detailing his experiences at Stelton, Gold came to the defense of the utopian project:

> Colonies are not scientific revolution; no, but they are a part of the art of revolution. They are direct action by the proletarian soul. They are as spontaneous, as inevitable, as useful and as beautiful as the writing of poetry. They are the poetry created by the hard hands of inspired workingmen, and whoever does not understand them, does not understand something that is in the heart of the proletarian.[16]

In the New York area, radicals created vacation colonies for adults. The Socialist-led International Ladies Garment Workers Union maintained Unity House in the Catskills, where their mostly Jewish and

Italian garment workers could take their families during the summer.[17] The Socialist Rand School in New York had Camp Tamiment,[18] and Communists organized Camp Nitgedaigit and Camp Unity, a few hours north of New York City.[19]

The shift in such practical expressions of utopianism from labor to leisure on the part of American radicals reached its fullest expression in the creation of children's summer camps in the 1920s. Radicals of all stripes organized children's summer programs to teach the values of their particular brand of radicalism and to realize, at least temporarily, some of their hopes for the future. Thus anarchists organized Camp Germinal in Pennsylvania; the socialist-oriented Jewish Workmen's Circle created Camp Kinderland and, when Kinderland was taken over by Communists, Camp Kinder Ring; and independent labor radicals organized Pioneer Youth camps in New York, North Carolina, and Pennsylvania.[20] The radical children's camps in the New York area were part of the rise of summer camping among Jews during the 1920s and 1930s. The New York Jewish community, a large but religiously and politically divided population, created numerous camps that reflected a wide variety of ideological and religious tendencies: camps were organized by religious groups and right-wing Zionists as well as the radicals.[21]

Summer camps for children organized by the Communists represented their utopian aspirations. Located throughout the United States, these camps were the focal point of the other aspects of the children's program, such as the after-school activities and the children's organizations. In the summer camps, children could be exposed to Communist values without the distractions of school or other non-Communist institutions, and the activities of the after-school programs and the children's organizations were often directed toward organizing for the camps.

Communists' construction of a vision of the future was grounded in their struggle to realize their political aims in the context of American culture. Because so many Communists were themselves immigrants, or had come from immigrant families, the relationship between the ethnic cultures of European immigrants and American culture, in general, was the context within which Communist political culture developed during the 1920s and 1930s.

Two aspects of the utopian current developed in the Communist political culture during this period. One had to do with he idealization of the Soviet Union and the other with the a projection for socialism in the United States. During the 1920s, these were often merged. The Communist slogan "For a Soviet America," the title of a book by William Z. Foster, illustrated the Communist view that socialism in the United States would mirror the experience of the Soviet Union. However, by the mid-1930s—especially, but not exclusively, after the turn toward the Popular Front—these two perspectives became more separate. Although the idealization of the Soviet Union remained, their goals for the United States became more an expression of a left-wing version of American democracy.

Three streams led into the river of the future American democracy as the Communists elaborated their vision during the late 1930s and 1940s. First was the role of labor. Unlike the "proletariat" of earlier Marxist perspectives, "labor" was less abstract: it was grounded in the struggles to organize the CIO industrial unions, rather than a more general, theoretical analysis. Yet "labor," too, was a theoretical construct—one that grafted the Marxist notion of the proletariat onto the American democratic "people." The "people" were to be represented by the CIO whether they actually be workers or, in fact, farmers, small-business people, or professionals. This joining of Jeffersonianism and Marxism allowed Communists to construct themselves as heirs to a popular radical tradition tracing back to the American Revolution.

A second stream was the reconfiguration of ethnicity. During the 1920s, American Communists hoped that the ethnic cultures and languages of the European immigrants would disappear, creating a working class with a shared American culture. The fight for socialism, they believed, could only be won within that shared culture. Ironically, unlike nonradicals who also looked toward the disappearance of ethnicity, Communists during this period had no love for American culture; they simply believed that revolutionary change would be impossible with a linguistically and ethnically divided working class. By the late 1930s, the perspective developed in the IWO came to prominence in Communist conceptions of the future of American democracy. Rather than a disappearance of ethnic culture, either through assimilation or through the "melting-pot" Communists came to project the IWO experience onto the country as a whole. America would be composed of many ethnic groups, each maintaining and celebrating the "progressive aspects of their national cultures, living in mutual respect with one another.

Democracy, in the Communist view, came to mean the right to difference and the projected a pluralist culture made up many different ethnic cultures.

Perhaps the most important aspect of the Communist construction of a utopian vision for America, that connected them to the reality of American history and culture, was also the arena in which Communists rejected the dominant strain in that culture. For the Communists race, in particular the role of African Americans in American society, marked the joining of their radicalism with their Americanism.

Beginning in 1928 with the Comintern decision on the importance of the African American struggle, Communists attempted to integrate support for the struggles of African Americans into their overall political perspective.[22] Their efforts to gain supporters among African Americans have been discussed by Mark Naison, writing about Harlem, Nell Painter, in her oral history/biography of Black Communist Hosea Hudson, and Robin Kelley, writing about Alabama.[23] Their work critiques earlier historical analyses of the relationship between the Communist Party and the African American community, such as that of Wilson Record, whose view that the Communists simply used struggles against racism for their own ends reflected the anti-Communism of the period in which it was written, and that of Harold Cruse, whose perspective was that the Communists inhibited the growth of an autonomous Black nationalism.[24] As these and other historians have pointed out, Communist efforts in this arena were complex and often ambiguous. For both Blacks and whites, however, the Communists articulated a vision of a nonracist America that went beyond equal rights.

Over the last thirty years, both historical analysis and American society have been transformed by the foregrounding of questions regarding women's participation in the workforce, politics, and society and, from this, by understandings regarding the construction of gender as a category of analysis. The Communist Party believed in women's equality, yet did not see it as central to its analysis of society or its political strategy. Furthermore, Communists during this period would have been surprised at contemporary uses of gender as a fundamental political category.

Nonetheless, the Communist perspective on the role of women developed from two contradictory streams. Drawing on Engels and

Bebel, Communists held that women were oppressed, as a group, and that this oppression originated with the development of private property; at the same time, they believed that capitalism exploited women as workers: women, like other groups, would be liberated as *part* of the working class with the creation of socialism. Historians have pointed out that the limits of Communist theory on women's social position lay in how, especially in light of contemporary feminism, the structure of Communist organization excluded women from leadership, and how the Communist vision of the working class was "masculinist," even though they engaged in campaigns with large numbers of women workers.[25] Communists also drew on a second, often contradictory, tradition that saw capitalism as the force that took women out of their roles as mothers and housewives.[26] Socialism, in this view, would return the natural gender order that capitalism had disrupted. Here the Communists, like many U.S. Socialists before them, valorized women's "natural" roles as mother and housekeeper. During the 1920s, when Communist rejection of bourgeois culture was more totalizing, Communists critiqued the family, and CP activity was a location for the construction of a culture of young female activists. Van Gosse has pointed out that the emergence of Popular Front Communism in the United States led to both a decrease in attention to women as potentially militant proletarian activists and an increase in the acceptance of more mainstream views on women's "sphere."[27]

However, gender rarely figured in the construction of the Communist vision of socialism outside idealization of the position of Soviet women. In the children's activities, gender never comes up. During the Young Pioneer period, both boys and girls are presented as potential leaders, and the activities the Pioneers were expected to engage in were nongendered. By the 1930s, in line with Van Gosse's analysis of the shift to more mainstream views on the position of women, there is a similar acceptance of difference in boys' and girls' activities. For example, as sports become more important, these activities are primarily for boys, while girls' activities tend toward the arts such as dance and drama.

The Marxist view of history is focused on the eternal struggle between the rich and the poor as it has been expressed throughout human experience. In every epoch, the poor had organized to overthrow their oppressors, and every time they were defeated. Even such victories as had occurred, such as the French Revolution or the Amer-ican Civil War, were limited or betrayed. For Communists, this was not a cause for despair, because they saw themselves standing at the cusp of this historical process. They were on the verge of the "final conflict," which would end with the complete victory of the poor and the oppressed. They themselves were to play the leading role in this great historical drama.

The particularistic and descriptive aspect of Marxism is its appeal to the modern working class as the central historical class in modern history, and to the "class-conscious" members of that class as the prime moving force within it. Marxism was thus able to provide radical immigrant workers with a sense of place in history that included both their own personal histories as workers and as immigrants and the history of the United States as a class society. Marxism further pointed toward the kinds of social action through which their assigned historical role could be carried out. It was this Marxist framework that connected the historical aspects of the political culture to the utopian aspects. Marxism provided both an interpretation of the past and a prediction of the future.

In their perspectives on the role of children in families and in society, and in the programs that they organized to give their children an alternative, oppositional culture, American Communists constructed a political culture of their own. This political culture provided a space in which the Communists could confront the tensions of their relationship with American society and with history.

the littlest proletariat

The Family, Child Rearing, and Education in Communist Theory, 1922–1934

Communists developed a unique perspective on child rearing, education, and family life during the 1920s and early 1930s as part of their effort to apply the Communist version of Marxism to the conditions of the American working class. They were not the first radicals to view the family through the lens of sociopolitical analysis. This discussion had been a feature of socialist theorizing since before Marx and Engels.

During the nineteenth and early twentieth centuries, socialists and other radicals debated between themselves and with conservatives the "politics" of the family, the prospects for a transformed family life "after the revolution," and the necessity of training children for the "new world." The Communists' perspective reflected their desire to formulate a "proletarian" approach to these issues based on their application of Marxism to U.S. conditions. They also drew upon the recurring debates in the international socialist movement since the days of Marx and Robert Owen—debates that continued in both the Communist International and in the traditions of the radical movements in the United States, particularly the Socialist and anarchist movements.

The Family in Communist Theory

When Communists entered into the theoretical discussion of the nature of the family under capitalism, they joined a discussion that had been a constant in socialist and radical movements since the early nineteenth century. The socialist debate on the family had been an arena in which some of the more utopian elements in socialist ideology were expressed, and, perhaps for this reason, attacks on socialist views of the family figured prominently in the arsenal of antisocialists.

Conservative critics of socialism often argued that the destruction of the nuclear family unit was an inevitable outcome of political radicalism. Like their opponents among the socialist critics of the family, conservatives believed that there was a direct connection between the political and domestic orders. However, rather than desiring this change, they feared that tampering with the political institutions would lead, necessarily, to the destruction of the family. Historian Sidney Ditzion wrote referring to this controversy: "Only recently [have] critics of socialism and its communist form ceased to link these political radicalisms as a matter of course with immorality and the destruction of the family. The two notions are still to be seen as an inseparable couplet in moves to discredit persons or movements."[1]

In fact, early-nineteenth-century utopian socialist theorists Robert Owen and Charles Fourier had argued that the rearrangement of family and child-rearing practices were an essential precondition for, or an accompaniment to, economic and political change. During the same period, utopian communities in the United States developed practices of family life along the lines indicated by their social philosophy. Thus, the group or "complex" marriage of the Oneida Community and the celibacy of the Shakers were attempts to transform the family to make it more compatible with these communities' utopian social theories. Marx and Engels felt compelled to take up the issue of the relationship between the family and socialism in *The Communist Manifesto*. Answering the charges of antisocialists that communists intended to destroy the family, Marx and Engels asserted that the capitalist system itself was the main antifamily force in contemporary society.[2] In his four-volume history of the American family, socialist historian Arthur Calhoun reiterated this position when he wrote: "The real menace to the family and home is not the doctrine of affinity proclaimed by sentimentalists nor yet the doctrine of free love but rather the relentless workings of the profit system."[3]

Yet the founders of Marxism were inconsistent in their views on the family, which allowed later socialist writers to speculate on possible forms the family might take under socialism. Friedrich Engels, in his *Origins of the Family, Private Property and the State,* connected the forms of family life practiced in each historical epoch to the mode of production dominant in that epoch. The epoch of socialism, he implied, might entail a new form of family life that would correspond to the new socialist mode of production.

Furthermore, Engels applied his analysis of power in capitalist society to power relations *within* the family. In Engels's discussion, as well as in those of the socialist writers who followed him, the critique of the family most often centered on the position of women. Engels argued that the structure of the contemporary family was predicated upon the subordination of women, and used the language of politics to describe the nature of this subordination: "The modern individual family is founded on the open or concealed domestic slavery of the wife. . . . Within the family he [the husband] is the bourgeois and the wife represents the proletariat."[4]

August Bebel, a founder and leader of the powerful German Social Democratic Party, and after Engels, was the most widely read socialist theoretician who dealt with the potential impact of socialism on the family. His *Woman under Socialism* was first published in Germany in 1883, and by the time of Bebel's death in 1913 had gone into more than fifty editions.[5] It was first published in the United States in an English translation in 1897, and by 1920 three new U.S. editions had appeared.[6] Bebel held that socialism would bring about the full equality of women, arguing that the subordination of women within the family and in society at large was based on the class divisions generated by capitalist relations of production. In his section entitled "Women in the Future," Bebel wrote that with socialism "class rule will have reached its end for all time, and along with it, the rule of man over woman."[7]

Bebel's projection of women's equality under socialism was not the most controversial part of his book; more radical was his belief that the implications of women's equality were the abolition of the family and the acceptance of the practice of "free love." He wrote:

> In the choice of love, she is, like man, free and unhampered. She woos or is wooed, and closes the bond from no considerations other than her own inclinations. . . .
>
> . . . *The satisfaction of the sexual instinct is as much a private concern as the satisfaction of any other natural instinct.* (emphasis in the original)[8]

Women under Socialism was among the most popular books in the German socialist movement.[9] This was not because the mass of German socialist workers were persuaded by Bebel's vision of free love under socialism. Rather, as Lewis Coser wrote in an introduction to a recent edition, it was because "millions of readers found here, in a simple and earthy language, arguments and facts that helped them articulate their diffuse and inchoate yearnings for a better world to come."[10] The popularity of *Women under Socialism* points to the strong connection between the utopian aspirations of socialists and the desire for domestic reorganization. John Spargo, one of the most able publicists of the Socialist Party of America and a critic of Bebel's views on the family, defended the socialist movement from the criticism that it was hostile to the family by distinguishing between modern "scientific" socialism and its utopian predecessors. In 1912, Spargo wrote: "Whatever hostility to marriage and the family had manifested itself in the course of the evolution of modern socialism has been incidental and accidental, a remnant of the old Utopian spirit."[11]

Although the socialist critique of family life most often focused on women's role in the family and society, antisocialists raised the issue of the effect of proposed changes in the family on children. Former socialist David Goldstein, a Catholic convert, wrote in 1903 in the antisocialist tract *Socialism: A Nation of Fatherless Children*: "The children? Yes, poor things, no doubt there shall be a measly lot of them under the new 'regime,' but all shall be orphaned. The community is to be father and mother of them all. The home having been absorbed by the 'household industries,' all the infants shall be turned out to grass in the pasture on the baby farms."[12] Later, in the famous debate between Socialist Party of America leader Morris Hillquit and the prominent Roman Catholic social reformer Father John A. Ryan (published as *Socialism: Promise or Menace?*), Father Ryan claimed that socialist animosity toward the family under capitalism would lead to the severing of ties between parents and children. ("The natural corollary to their doctrine of 'marriage for love,' Socialists subscribe more or less generally and definitely to the theory that the child belongs to the State."[13])

The antisocialist emphasis on the relationship between mothers and children was not foreign to Socialists like John Spargo. His rejection of Bebel's vision of free love and socialism placed him firmly among those who sought to defend the ideal family of the nineteenth century from the ravages of capitalism. In his sentimental paean to motherhood, *Socialism and Motherhood*, Spargo wrote that the natural bond between mother and child should not be tampered with: "From time to time, amiable theorists—generally childless—have propounded plans for supplanting the individual mother in the rearing of children. All sorts of communal nurseries with 'scientific direction and management' have been advocated. . . . All observed facts go to show that it is insanity for a child to be deprived of the attention of its mother."[14] Further, in this work Spargo links his acceptance of the prevailing idealization of the family with a vision of the socialist future: "Socialism, then, is an attempt to realize in the larger life of the community that rational and fair adjustment of collective and individual power and responsibility that is exemplified by the family at its best."[15]

The nineteenth-century division between the morality of the home and that of the marketplace gave critics of capitalism such as Spargo a place to stand within the mainstream culture, and at the same time afforded them a basis for proposing an alternative to the dominance of commercial values. Spargo shared this perspective with Francis Willard, the head and symbol of the Women's Christian Temperance Union, perhaps the largest and most influential women's organization of this time.[16] Willard became a socialist because, for her, socialism offered the most thorough defense of traditional feminine values against the pressures of capitalism: "Were I to define in a sentence the thought and purpose of the Women's Christian Temperance Union, I would reply: *It is to make the whole world* homelike [emphasis in the original]."[17]

The difficulty that the socialist writers on the family faced in finding a place for children in the new social order opened them up to the kinds of criticisms made by Father Ryan and David Goldstein. For Bebel and other socialist advocates of a transformed family life, the raising of children often figured as one of the responsibilities of the family that, like laundry and cooking, could be taken over by social institutions. On the other hand, socialists who, like Willard and Spargo, saw the family as a center of values in opposition to capitalism, were bound by nineteenth-century convention to a sentimentalized vision of domestic and social harmony that was essentially that of the middle class. The Communist rejection of both Socialist analyses of the family was the result of internal developments in radical ideology and

the transformation of American family life that occurred in the first
two decades of the twentieth century.

A Working-Class Childhood: Poverty, Labor,
and Autonomy

To develop a "proletarian" perspective on childhood, Communists
began in the conditions in which working-class children and their families lived. Communists focused on the poverty and social crisis that
were part of so many working-class children's lives, and the ways these
conditions were created by capitalism.

The daily grind of poverty and exploitation suffered by working-
class families belied the halcyon image portrayed in sentimental versions of the family. The Communists contested the bourgeois perception of childhood innocence. They viewed the belief that childhood was
a stage of life outside of social and historical struggles as a mask for the
exploitation of working-class children; the "struggle for existence" was
constant in the experiences of working-class children. Far from being
protected from economic reality by their families, the working-class
family was the focal point for children's class experiences.

Working-class mothers and fathers were beset with worries about providing basic necessities. These concerns greatly strained family relations
and contributed to conflict between family members. Children's experiences of the parents' inability to control their family's economic position
were seen as a corollary to the overall political powerlessness of the working class. Working-class children were further confronted by their own
direct oppression—by child labor, poor schools, and unhealthy neighborhoods. The economic victimization of children, both indirectly through
the exploitation of their parents and directly through their own difficult
conditions, remained central to the ways Communists viewed children
during the first decade of Communist Party children's activities.[18]

The focus of Communist analysis of capitalism during the 1920s was
that misery and social powerlessness were characteristic of working-
class life. Communists believed that the "prosperity" of that decade was
a sham—one that never extended to the working class.[19] The onset of
the Great Depression in 1929 reinforced, for the Communist Party, its
view that working-class misery was an inherent characteristic of capi-

talism. Indeed, during the Depression ever greater numbers of working-class children lived in conditions that reflected what had been the
Communist analysis of the position of children in capitalist society since
the early 1920s.

Economist Grace Hutchins, in her book *Children Under Capitalism*,
published in 1932, examined the problems faced by working-class children in the Depression-era from a Communist perspective. She emphasized both the direct and indirect aspects of children's economic victimization in the midst of the Great Depression. Her first sentences—"I
saw a baby die of undernourishment. His father is a longshoreman,
earning 67 cents an hour, but he has only a few hours' work in the
week"—seemed intended to shock readers into a recognition of how
bad things were for working-class families.[20]

Later, in an another example of the effects of unemployment and
poverty on working-class children, Hutchins related the story of Eugene
Olsen, a New York City high school student whose suicide had been the
subject of a *New York Times* story in June 1932. The father had been out
of work and the family had been evicted from their apartment to live in
a basement storeroom. The father said that the only reason he could give
for the boy's suicide was worry over their financial condition.[21]

These descriptions of deprivation highlighted conditions that were
known by non-Communist commentators as well. In *Human Aspects of
Unemployment and Relief*, James Mickel Williams of Hobart College
reported an increase in child malnutrition in New York City from 18 percent in 1928 to 60 percent during the Great Depression, and an increase
from 18 percent in the 1929/30 school year to 27 percent in 1932.[22]

At the same time as massive unemployment among their parents
defined working-class experience for many children, child labor
remained widespread during this period. Hutchins cited the 1930 census,
which listed more than two million workers under the age of seventeen
and more than 660,000 of that number between the ages of ten and fif-
teen. She noted that this number seriously underestimated the extent to
which child labor was practiced in the United States by leaving out children engaged in agricultural work.[23] Indeed, in 1940 the National Child
Labor Committee estimated that there remained 750,000 to 900,000 children employed two years after federal legislation outlawing child labor,
most of them in occupations excluded from legal protection and working
in agriculture and "street trades."[24]

Opposition to child labor meant something different to the Communists than it did to the reformers. Communists opposed child labor for many of the same reasons that the reformers did; at the same time they viewed child laborers as a specially exploited section of the working class. Because the class identity of child workers was formed through their own relationship to labor, not only through their familial relationship to adult workers, Communists believed that child workers could be brought to class consciousness through mechanisms similar to those used with adults, and that, similarly, children needed the protection of trade unions. The Young Pioneers often called for unionization of child workers as a response to the conditions of working-class childhood, and Communist publications noted children's participation in strikes. For example, when *Workers Life,* the publication of Workers International Relief (WIR), reported on a strike in the beet fields of Colorado in 1932, it noted that child agricultural workers, some as young as five or six years old, went on strike with their parents.[25]

Changes in working-class family life during the end of the nineteenth and beginning of the twentieth centuries were transforming these children's relationship to their parents. At the turn of the century, traditional patriarchal authority remained at the core of rural family life. It was necessary for the entire family to contribute to production.[26] At the same time, middle-class children were increasingly connected to their parents by bonds of affection, while extended education led to a longer period of financial dependency.[27] Urban working-class childhood differed significantly from that of middle-class children in the proportion of children's lives spent away from parental influence and authority. In cities, the streets were a world of children. Newsies, bootblacks, and other children labored in the streets at the same time that increasing numbers of children, unencumbered by the necessity of working, were using the streets for play. In his book *Children of the City at Work and at Play,* David Nasaw wrote that "children at play inhabited a world that was encased in but separate from the ordinary adult world that surrounded them."[28]

The autonomy of working-class children was an issue for both the child-labor reformers and those urban progressives who began to organize institutions to control children's street lives, or to remove them from the streets altogether.[29] Nasaw wrote that "the child labor reformers and their allies feared for the street traders not because they were exposed to physical danger or deprived of sensory stimulation or physically confined during daylight hours. They set out to save them from a different order of evils: from too much, not too little freedom, stimulation and excitement."[30]

In confronting these issues, Communists were influenced by an American debate that had emerged during the progressive reform period of the late nineteenth and early twentieth century. Middle-class reformers had been concerned with the effects of industrial society on children and had attempted to remedy what they perceived to be the most grievous of these effects. Progressives campaigned to both end child labor and to socialize working-class children into middle-class mores. Communists often shared with the middle-class social reformers a concern with the social degradation associated with urban life. A pamphlet issued by the Young Communist International railed that the streets in which working-class children lived were "a great foul gutter thru which passes all the scum of capitalist society."[31] In language that could have come from the pen of a middle-class social reformer, the pamphlet described the dangers of urban life for a working-class child: "In the public houses and brothel districts, he comes into contact with vice in every form. The cheap picture shows with their rude posters appeal to all his lower instincts."[32] However, the pamphlet's solution was not to increase the control of adults or the middle class over working-class children; it was to elaborate organizational structures in which the autonomy of working-class children could be directed toward revolutionary ends. Neither the family nor the schools could be counted upon to develop revolutionary consciousness in children. Communist analysis of the role of the family in capitalist society and of the potential of Communist education emerged from the Communists view of the lives of working-class children and their belief that developing revolutionary class consciousness in children was the only way that solutions to their problems could be found.

Edwin Hoernle, a German Communist and author of *A Manual for Leaders of Children's Groups,* published by the Young Communist International, wrote: "It is sad but true that today the attitude of proletarian parents—even communist parents—to the children . . . is still purely bourgeois and based on paternal power."[33] This point was made in stronger terms by the authors of the Young Communists' *The Child of the Worker*: "Very often the family of some otherwise revolutionary comrade is the last refuge of the evil practices of the petty bourgeoisie and of egoistic tyranny. How many a worker while a slave in the factory uses in his own home the manners of a despot?"[34] Although these two works were first published in Europe, they influenced Young Pioneer leaders in the United States, according to Ernest Rymer, the national director of the Young Pioneers of America during the late 1920s. Both were translated into English and sold in Communist bookstores in the United States,[35] and sections of the manual were reprinted in the newsletter of the junior section of the Young Workers League.[36]

Many of those who became Communists during the 1920s had grown up in the streets of America's cities, and their experiences shaped their analysis of childhood and their views of the family. They emphasized the autonomous nature of childhood and saw in this autonomy the key to the development of revolutionary consciousness in children. Although their conception of the political necessity for children's autonomy reflected the Communists' perspective on the politics of the family, it also drew upon a recognition that the lives of urban working-class children allowed a great deal of autonomy from parents and, often, other forms of adult authority as well. While Engels had used a metaphor for class struggle to describe women's position within the family, Communists in the 1920s used that metaphor to illustrate the powerlessness of children. In Engels's view, women were the "proletariat" in relationship to the "bourgeois" power of their husbands; in the view of the Communist Children's Movement, children were a little "proletariat" in relation to the authority and power of their parents and the adult world.

Socialist Education, Proletarian Education, and the Communist Children's Movement

Communists, like many other Americans in the first half of the twentieth century, were concerned that the role of the family in the socialization of children was being undermined due to the growing importance of extrafamilial influences on children. The most important influence on working-class children, outside the family and the street, was the school. Communists believed that the school represented interests opposed to those of the working class; its job was to inculcate children with conservative values and to teach them to support the status quo. As *The Child of the Worker* expressed it: "What is the character of the present day school?

It is an institution of the ruling classes for the poisoning of the working-class children, an institution for the training of servile and submissive wage slaves, a nursery for future scabs and white guards."[37]

The problem of how to educate children so that they would grow up to be radicals animated much radical thinking on education beginning in the nineteenth century. By the latter part of that century, socialist and anarchist thinking on education was often directed toward the problems of transmitting the values of the socially divergent and politically dissenting views of radical parents to their children. Communist ideas on education came out of this earlier discussion and drew upon both socialist and anarchist educational ideas and practices; at the same time, Communists attempted to develop a Communist-oriented educational practice that differed from that of their radical predecessors.

The educational theories and organizational practices directed toward inculcating radical political ideas in children were connected to radical critiques of public education, for radicals believed that both the form and content of traditional schooling had a conservative orientation; however, the radical critique of public schooling was often concerned with issues of access and the role of education in the reproduction of the class structure. The development of programs for children by the radical movement was often seen as augmenting public education, or providing alternatives to it that were directed toward the desires of the radical parents to provide for their children instruction in the culture of the radical movement.

American radicals had long been sympathetic to the philosophy of "free" or "rationalist" education propounded by the early nineteenth-century Swiss educational reformer Johann Heinrich Pestalozzi. Pestalozzi had criticized the emphasis on "rote" learning, discipline, and classical training that was characteristic of most education of his time. He argued for a more experimental and scientific form of education in which the natural curiosity of the child would be encouraged. The schools in Robert Owen's New Harmony community were organized around Pestalozzi's theories, and the Swiss reformer's ideas influenced both the later "progressive" educational theories associated with John Dewey and the anarchist educational theory of Francisco Ferrer. Radicals in the United States were attracted to this tradition because they perceived traditional education as preparing children for lives of obedience, and therefore inuring children to radical ideas about society.

At the same time, radicals saw themselves as competing directly with the political conservatism that they perceived to be common in both the public school curricula and religious Sunday schools. By the twentieth century, Dewey's elaboration of Pestalozzi's ideas was accepted by most Socialist educational thinkers. Historian Jocelyn Tien, writing about the educational ideas held by American socialists, noted: "During the first two decades of the twentieth century, those in the Socialist movement who were interested in education and who wrote about it were almost unanimous in espousing the principles of progressive education."[38]

The influence of Progressive educational ideas was also felt in the Socialist Sunday schools organized by Socialists before the First World War; there, Socialists attempted to put their educational ideas into practice.[39] For example, Samuel Slavsky, a teacher in the Sunday schools, said in a newspaper interview in 1919:

> Everything done in our "Sunday Schools" is devoid of narrow academicism; a spirit of bigness, of the cosmic, is brought into the atmosphere.
>
> Freedom of expression is substituted for the impressive and constraining influences brought to bear on children by the existing educational system. The teachers are unbiased and the children are learning to be likewise.[40]

Unlike most advocates of progressive education, radical educators were also concerned with the ideological content of the curriculum. Experimental educational methods were not, to them, ends in themselves, but means toward teaching radical political ideology to children. Thus the Socialist journal of education, the *Progressive Journal of Education*, contained articles on teaching the Marxist interpretation of American history and on the importance of vocational education, as well as articles by John Dewey on educational methods.[41]

Although everyone involved in radical educational activities, whether Socialist or anarchist, wanted children to enjoy participation in their educational programs, there were significant differences as to how much political content was thought to be important and how that content should actually be taught. Some Socialist Sunday schools drew more upon the tradition of the religious Sunday schools, and their organizers saw their primary task as competing with the religious Sunday schools. For example, the Rochester Socialist Sunday school was one of the more successful organized before the First World War. Part of the regular curriculum was the singing of Socialist hymns put to popular tunes of the day, Socialist catechisms, and even Socialist prayers. Kendrick Shedd, the leading figure in the Rochester school, wrote: "Socialist Sunday Schools are conducted much the same as capitalist Sunday schools."[42]

Even among Socialists sympathetic to the aims of the Socialist Sunday school movement there were reservations about the extent to which Socialist ideology could be taught to children. David Berenberg, who taught a course on education at the Socialist Rand School for Social Science in New York City, questioned whether Socialism was actually being taught in the Socialist Sunday schools. He wrote in an article in the *Socialist World* in 1920:

> Some have sought to teach "Socialism" to immature children, entirely overlooking the fact that "Socialism" as a system of political thought presupposes a great deal of historical knowledge, and requires a thorough understanding of economics. Other schools, in an endeavor to avoid the dogmatic teaching of Socialism, have taught a watery reformism or a stupid and incorrect version of evolution and anthropology, totally unrelated to Socialism.[43]

Anarchist educators were more consistent in their rejection of the authoritarianism characteristic of public school and religious Sunday school education. Not content simply to replace capitalist with anticapitalist indoctrination, anarchists believed that educational practice should embody their ideals of freedom and autonomy; thus, they were forced to confront the problem that the children exposed to "free" education might not develop the political ideology of their parents.

In the aftermath of the execution of the Spanish anarchist educator Francisco Ferrer, American anarchists and anarchist sympathizers created a network of educational institutions for children known as "modern schools"—named after Ferrer's Escuela Moderna in Barcelona. There were "modern" Sunday schools as well as full-day alternative schools.[44] The most successful "modern school" was the one at Stelton, New Jersey, which lasted as an anarchist community and school from 1916 to 1958.[45] In these schools, the conflict between "free" education and radical "political" socialization was constantly debated. At Stelton, the directors of the school were committed to nonindoctrinating education, and were ever warding off attempts by parents to have a more politically oriented curriculum taught the children.

The attraction of radicals to the rationalist, experimental tradition in education represented by Pestalozzi and, later, Dewey was rooted both in their critique of schooling per se in capitalist society and in their understanding of how radicalization occurred, even among adults. They tended to see radical ideology as an objective assessment of the problems of society; radicalism was, thus, a perspective in which the world was understood realistically and without prejudice. "Free" education would allow children to view the world without the constraints of conservative bias, and therefore lead them to radical ideology on their own. Benzion Liber, a Rumanian immigrant doctor associated with the "modern school" movement, defended this view of education in his book *The Child and the Home:*

> Rational education of children would allow free course to the child's questions and would let his logical thinking and reasoning go to their extreme, indifferent to the consequences. Perhaps the child would then discover how deeply immoral and corrupt society is, perhaps he would find out the true meaning of commerce, of capital, of war, of charity, of riches, of inheritance. Perhaps he would ask himself or he would ask us, why the land, which has certainly not been made by anybody, is owned by some people and not by others. . . . Perhaps the mystery of this complicated but profoundly unsound society would unfold itself before him and he would see how deeply it is immersed in theft and all that ensues from it.[46]

Radicals of many stripes held to this view—that their ideology was based on a rationalist, objective perspective on society and its institutions, and believed that children exposed to education based on these principles would come to radicalism on their own. In addition, they did not believe that there could be any possible contradiction between their view of the world and one arrived at freely by children if the facts were explained to them. Historian Avvo Kostiainen describes an article that appeared in the Finnish Socialist paper *Tovaritar* entitled "The Class Education of Our Children." The piece laid out radicals' assumptions that properly educated children would inevitably develop revolutionary consciousness: "Class relations, as well as other social questions, must be continuously explained to the children. And when the facts had been presented to them, it was claimed, the children themselves would voluntarily accept socialist ideas."[47]

Communists were initially more sympathetic to the efforts of the anarchists than to the Socialist Sunday schools, in part reflecting the mutual sympathy that existed between anarchists and Communists in the first years of the Russian Revolution. Anarchists and Communists shared an antagonism toward reformist socialism and a sympathy for the Russian Revolution.[48] William Thurston Brown had been a founder of the "modern school" movement and director of the Stelton school for three years before moving on in 1919 to organize a similar school in Los Angeles. Like others among the anarchists, he became a Bolshevik sympathizer, and until he died in 1938 he was an activist in pro-Soviet organizations.[49] Comparing the activities of the school at Stelton to the efforts of the Bolsheviks in Russia, Brown wrote:

> The Ferrer School, or the Ferrer kind of school, is for the schools what the Russian democracy is for the rest of the nations—all of them, this as well as the rest. Politically we have been saying: "We can't go any faster than political and industrial evolution permits us. We cannot hale Utopia on by force—we can only follow the path of historical development."
>
> They [the Bolsheviks] know themselves as the most essential factor in evolution. They have vision, imagination, energy, youth, boundless courage, infinite daring, resolute determinism—before such things traditions fade like mists before the sun.[50]

Two Communist writers from England, Eden and Cedar Paul, also commented favorably on the Stelton modern school in their book on the development of proletarian culture, *Proletcult*. The Stelton school was, they wrote, "a self-governing school for proletarian children . . . under proletarian control, and . . . imbued with the proletarian spirit. At the same time it is extraordinarily advanced in its pedagogic methods, the education being guided by the discoveries of the New Psychology. . . . We doubt whether a finer example of a Proletcultural school can be found even in Soviet Russia."[51] However, Hugo Gellert, the Communist artist who had taught at the Stelton school in its early years, reflected during the 1930s that he thought anarchist parents had been untrue to themselves and their children by not taking the children "into full confidence" about their political beliefs, and saw this as a reason for so few children from these schools growing up to be radicals.[52]

As Communists developed their own ideology distinct from that of their radical predecessors, they became increasingly critical of both anarchist and Socialist models of education for children. An editorial in *The Worker's Child*, a Communist journal for leaders of children's organizations, took issue with laissez-faire ideas about raising children to be radicals that had been common among socialist and anarchist parents.

> Parents often ask why they should organize their children. "Isn't it enough," they ask, "that we are active? Let the child grow up without being influenced by me. When he grows up he will decide for himself."
>
> This is arguing against our own children. Our children are not excluded by kind capitalists from being exploited. . . . As for letting our children grow up without being influenced so they can later decide "impartially" for themselves, that is impossible. The bourgeoisie shape our children's minds with the schools, radio, movies, newspapers, etc. Every day their children's organizations, like the Boy Scouts, work to turn our children against us by giving them a strike-breaking, militarist ideology.[53]

Communists attempted to forge a link between the anarchist tradition in education, in which the educational practices themselves reflected a radical view of the world, and the Socialist tradition, in which the content of radical education was primary. They reserved their strongest criticisms for the reformist Socialist tradition, while at the same time proposing that Communist children's activities should have a more conscious political direction than the anarchist schools. Hoernle, the German author, criticized the Socialist schools and articulated a theoretical connection between Communist politics and educational practice:

> We differ from those friends of education who believe that "new men must be educated; that children should be taught to love justice and truth and brotherly consideration in the present capitalist society." We differ also from those people who believe that children should learn Communism by heart, in "proletarian Sunday schools." We stand for revolutionary class education. . . . We do not teach the children ready-made formulae and dogma. We only make their natural instincts conscious forces.[54]

The structure of the Communist children's organizations was to be different from both the anarchist and the Socialist children's schools.

Rather than being simply educational institutions, controlled by parents and local party organizations, the Communist children's groups were to be political organizations, fully integrated into the political structure of the party. Communist children's groups would thus encourage children to engage in political as well as educational activity, and these groups would be separate from direct parental influence. Nat Kaplan, the national junior director of the Young Worker's League, emphasized that the crucial difference between the Communist children's organizations and those of earlier radical organizations was that the Communists expected children to be politically active in the revolutionary movement. He wrote: "Let us remember that it is mainly on this point that we differ from the old form of child organization—the worker's Sunday schools. We are not only preparing the child for future participation in the class struggle;—we are leading the child in the class struggle now!"[55]

The application of adult models of political organization to children in the Communist children's groups was neither a rejection of the earlier Socialist and anarchist educational models nor simply a repudiation of the bourgeois sentimental views of childhood innocence; it was the way that Communists located in their children's organizations their own utopian hopes and expectations. Unlike the earlier radicals, they saw the basis of socialist education in political practice. Thus, Communist children's organizations had to be more than educational institutions in the traditional sense; they had to be actual political organizations struggling for the improvement of the lives of working-class children: among the demands raised by the Young Pioneers during the 1920s and early 1930s were the abolition of child labor, playgrounds for city children, and free school lunches. At the same time, they believed that, in more fully separating the children from the world of their parents, they could create a model of what the socialist community would look like in the children's organizations. As Hoernle wrote: "It is necessary to find a form of organization which is governed by neither individual egoism nor by the herd spirit; one that stimulates the highest form of activity and of solidarity. This organization is the free, self-administered, and the self-legislative children's group."[56] Hoernle went on to say that "a new relation between adults and children is developing not in homes of the proletariat, but in the children's groups. . . . Inside them the life is that of a completely free community."[57]

COMMUNISM, EDUCATION, AND ETHNICITY

To Communists, education was primarily an effort to confront the social and ideological problems of raising their own children to follow in their political footsteps. It was in this effort that they faced the issue of the role of ethnicity, both in U.S. life in general and in the radical movement in particular. Most Communists during the 1920s were immigrants, and they wanted to preserve their cultures in the face of the pressures toward Americanization. They understood American culture to be hostile to their ideas and values and saw Americanization as a way of drawing their children away from them. To the consternation of their parents, the children of immigrant Communists were, indeed, becoming Americanized. However, the Communist Party, as an organization, supported Americanization as a way of reaching beyond the borders of the ethnic enclaves where its strongest support was. This contradiction—between the belief that Americanization would be beneficial to the radical movement and the desires of immigrant radical parents to transmit their ethnic cultures to their children—framed much of the discussion of Communist education, as it had framed a similar discussion for earlier radicals. The question of whether the children would carry on the radical values of their immigrant parents while shedding much of the ethnic culture in which that radicalism had been nurtured was a crucial issue in Communist thinking; it was also crucial in the development of Communist children's activities.

Such an issue was not, of course, limited to Communists: all immigrants to the United States were concerned about the cultural differences that emerged between their American-born children and themselves. Some immigrant leaders, including some socialists, echoed the demands of native-born Americanizers that immigrants should drop their European cultures and adopt American ones. However, most immigrants attempted to maintain the national cultures of their European homelands by building and supporting churches and synagogues, creating programs for the instruction of children in their native language, celebrating traditional feasts and holidays, and remaining actively involved in the political affairs of their countries of origin.[58] For radical immigrants of the period between the 1880s and the 1920s, the conflict was felt particularly acutely because of their political critique of capitalist society. They perceived, perhaps correctly, that American culture, in general, was a manifestation of bourgeois ideology.

Immigrants predominated in the socialist movement during the latter part of the nineteenth and early twentieth centuries, in part because they were an increasingly large proportion of the working class as a whole and in part because the kinds of radicalisms, particularly Marxian socialism, that flourished in immigrant communities were rooted in the European working-class movement. Socialist politics and ethnic cultures developed together in immigrant communities: immigrant radicals created their own institutions and organizations dedicated to both preserving native languages and cultures and to strengthening their communities' radical and labor movements. In this context, socialist parents in the United States often perceived the Americanization of their children as a challenge to their socialist values.

The problem of Americanization became an important issue in the discussion of children's political socialization and education because of the predominantly immigrant character of the Socialist—and later the Communist—movement. The concern of immigrant radicals for their children's upbringing was intertwined with the fear aroused by the cultural differences between them and their American-born children. In 1898, social reformer Mary Kingsbury commented on this connection in the Jewish immigrant working-class community. She wrote, optimistically, that socialism had proved to be a means of overcoming the cultural gaps between immigrant parents and their American children. Her comments highlight an issue that was of vital concern to Socialists, and, later, Communists: the situation when the parents were immigrants and the children were not:

> One of the most dramatic situations in the Ghetto, that home of pathos and drama, is the separation that so often arises between members of the same family . . . due to Americanization. . . .
>
> Socialism of course does not prove a conserving force where it is held by the child alone, but where both father and child are socialists, the unlovely sight of a dismembered family is not exhibited; the family bond is secure.[59]

Benzion Liber noted that the relationship between the development of radical politics and generational change in Europe—in which children could be expected to be more radical than their parents—had been reversed in the United States. "This can be explained," he wrote, "by the fact that the parents were converted to their ideas in Europe or in this country among their fellow-countrymen, while their children have been abandoned completely to the influence of the Americanizing school, which often means a reactionary influence."[60]

It was in response to these problems that the socialist movement organized the Socialist Sunday schools, the first of the efforts by American socialists to provide an institutional setting for the transmission of radical values from parents to children. The earliest of these Socialist Sunday schools were socialist versions of the nonpolitical or church-related children's programs that flourished in most of the immigrant communities at the turn of the century. The German Socialists were very active in this area, and the *Young Socialist Magazine*, the journal of the Socialist Sunday school movement, contained at least two pages in German until 1917.[61]

Overall, among the new immigrants of the late nineteenth century, Socialism was strongest among Eastern European Jews and Finns. The socialist children's programs created in these communities reflected the particular features of the radical movement in these groups. The preservation of language and culture was central to Finnish children's programs, among both the Socialists and Communists; however, Eastern European Jewish Socialists debated the relationship between ethnic identity and Socialist consciousness, framing the discussion in terms of support or opposition to cultural assimilation. Parts of this debate began in the Jewish communities of Eastern Europe during the nineteenth century, and it continued through the post–World War II period among Jewish radicals of all stripes in the United States, including Communists.

Jewish radicalism in the United States was centered in New York City and grew as a result of the experience of so many of these immigrants in the sweated needle trades there. At first, Jewish radicals in the United States were almost uniformly proponents of cultural assimilation. They believed that the maintenance of separate religious and secular traditions, including the use of the Yiddish language, was an outmoded reflection of the enforced isolation of Jews from the mainstream of Western culture and civilization. They identified with the tradition of Enlightenment rationalism and held as a goal the complete integration of Jews into the cultures in which they lived. To them, the effort to radicalize the Jewish working class was dependent on ending the distinctions between Jews and other workers. Thus when the Workmen's Circle, a Jewish fraternal benefit society, organized their first children's Sunday schools in 1906, instruction was in English, with Socialism, rather than Jewish culture, at the center of the curriculum.[62]

At the same time, there was another, smaller trend, among Jewish Socialists that emphasized the Jewish nature of the immigrants' radicalism and saw the Yiddish language both as the common means of expression of the Jewish working class and as the cultural basis for a secular Jewish form of radicalism. This trend was represented by the Poale Zion, a socialist Zionist organization, the National Jewish Worker's Alliance, and by "the Bund," which had been very influential in Europe.[63] The Bund, as the General Jewish Workers Union of Poland and Lithuania was known, had been the largest radical organization among Jews in the Russian Empire. It rejected both Zionism and Socialist assimilationism in favor of a socialism based on the social and cultural autonomy of Jews, wherever they lived. Although many immigrant Jewish socialist leaders had been Bundists in Europe, many of them, in the United States, initially moved to an assimilationist position.

In the conflict between assimilationists and anti-assimilationists in the Jewish socialist movement, the anti-assimilationists most represented the ideas of the Jewish working-class constituency. The growth of the Yiddish-language *Daily Forward* as the voice of Jewish socialism and of the Jewish community in New York was a sign of the dominance of the Yiddishist/culturalist position among Jewish socialists. The *Daily Forward* was both an ethnic newspaper reporting on the daily travails and triumphs of the immigrant community and a vehicle that propounded socialism in a language and idiom accessible to its readers.

The rejection of assimilationism by the Jewish immigrant working class in New York transformed the Jewish socialist educational institutions. Between 1910 and 1916, participation in the schools of the Workmen's Circle declined drastically, and many Workmen's Circle members were dissatisfied with the assimilationist emphases in the curriculum.[64] In 1916, the educational committee of the Workmen's Circle issued a report calling for an increased Jewish emphasis in the schools, saying: "Our children are growing up alien to our language, to the ideals and customs of our people. They look down upon the majority of our people . . . as an inferior culture! Occasionally, their attitude is that of contempt. . . . Our children should be acquainted with the immense treasures of Jewish culture."[6] The change in emphasis, toward the development of ethnic culture, led the schools of the Workmen's Circle to spearhead the process by which Yiddish-language instruction and Jewish culture became seen as important to radical educational efforts among children in the Jewish community. Even after the split between Communists and Socialists in the organization during the 1920s, both sides continued this emphasis on the preservation of the Jewish heritage.

Unlike the Eastern European Jews, Finnish radicals were almost unanimous in their belief in the maintenance of their language and ethnic cultural traditions. Socialist Finnish immigrants focused their movement on the Finnish immigrant community, and much of their activity was conducted through the Finnish Socialist Federation, one of the largest foreign-language federations affiliated with the Socialist Party. Finnish socialism became known as "Hall Socialism," because so much of the efforts of the Socialist movement went toward cultural activities that took place in Finn "halls" built in almost every Finnish community in America. These activities included Socialist choruses, dramatic groups, consumer cooperatives, and extensive children's activities, almost all conducted in Finnish.[66] Prior to 1920, Finnish Socialists published regular children's journals, annual spring and Christmas magazines, and a Socialist reader for children, all in Finnish.[67]

For both Finnish and Jewish Socialists who became Communists during the 1920s, ethnicity and radicalism remained interrelated. Nonetheless, the Communist Party was initially far less sympathetic to ethnic autonomy than the Socialist Party had been, as was shown in its abolition of the Communist foreign-language federations in 1928, in the hope that immigrant Communists would transfer their allegiance to an "American," multiethnic organization. In particular, the Communists hoped that English-speaking children of immigrant Communists would be the ones to facilitate the Americanization of the movement. Thus, during the 1920s the branch of the Young Pioneers in the Brownsville section of Brooklyn was told that it could no longer conduct its meetings in Yiddish, even though this was the primary language of most of the membership.[68] This conflict was even more intense among Finnish Communists. When the Finnish Worker's Federation of the Worker's Party was dissolved, the Communist Party lost much support among

Finnish radicals—support that it could ill afford to lose because the Finns provided a great deal of the Communist Party's financial support during these early years.

The changing relationship between ethnicity and radical politics between the 1920s and 1930s was at the heart of changes in the Communist children's organizations' approach to child rearing and family life. During the 1920s, the Communist Party had hoped to convince its members and sympathizers that identification with American life was crucial to the efforts to build an American revolutionary movement. Immigrant radicals and their families were expected to exchange their ethnic identifications for an identification with the Communist movement and the working class as a whole. By the mid-1930s, the party became more accepting of the ethnic ties of so many of its sympathizers and began to recognize the importance of the links between ethnic identification and political radicalism. Although this change was associated with the emergence of the Popular Front strategy during the mid-1930s, the change in the general strategy of the Communist Party only served to legitimate, in the children's organizations, practices that had been occurring since the beginning.

It was often those Communists active in the children's organizations, and Communist parents, that pressed for a change in the Communist attitude toward ethnicity. They were the closest to the desires of Communist parents to transmit ethnic as well as political values to the children.[69] Communists who were immigrants or children of immigrants were unwilling to accept the formulation that revolutionary ideology and Americanization went hand in hand: it both went against their feelings about their own place in American society and seemed contrary to their political analysis of American culture. They believed that one of the purposes of the Communist children's programs was to protect their children from the influences of American society, not to serve as a force for acculturation.

By the mid-1930s, the Communist Party had reconciled itself to the perception among many of its supporters that revolutionary politics could be linked to ethnic identification. The International Workers Order, which had been founded in 1930 as a federation of Communist-led ethnic fraternal benefit societies, had become the major organization responsible for children's activities in the Communist movement. The IWO's respect for and encouragement of ethnic identification among both children and adults was reflected in a changed view of family life and the role of politics in child rearing. Instead of emphasizing the conflicts between parents and children, and the necessity for children to develop political consciousness separately from their parents, the IWO saw the radical family as a unit. Max Bedacht, a founder of the Communist Party and general secretary of the IWO throughout the 1930s, wrote: "Every organizer and leader of the Order must therefore see the need of providing a field where children can work and learn and be active together with their parents, for the same objectives of their parents and in the spirit of their parents."[70]

The Communists came to recognize that the revolutionary socialization of children best took place in the context of their families, not in opposition to them. Whereas during the 1920s the family was seen by Communist writers as a microcosm of class society as a whole, during the mid-1930s this was changed: the working-class family was seen as a microcosm of the working class. In the first view, as the society was characterized by class struggle, so was the family characterized by generational struggle; in the second view, as the working class must overcome internal divisions to confront the main enemy of capitalism, so, too, must the working-class family be united. Jerry Trauber, national director of the IWO junior section, wrote in 1938 that "our education aims at creating the same unity within the working-class family that should exist within the working class as a whole."[71]

During the 1920s and the early 1930s, Communist writers on the education and socialization of children and on children's relationship to their families had focused on two interrelated issues: the necessity for children to engage in conscious political activity and the need for children to develop revolutionary consciousness apart from the direct influence of their parents. By the mid-1930s, this perspective had altered. It resulted from the persistence of ethnic identification among immigrant Communists and from the recognition that ethnic identification and revolutionary ideology were not necessarily incompatible. In fact, in the context of the United States they were intricately connected.

These themes—the relationships between ethnic culture and American culture and between working-class and bourgeois consciousness—dominated the discussion of Communist children's activities from the 1920s through the 1940s. Whereas during the first period (1922–1934) the emphasis was on identifying Communist political culture with an international working-class culture, during the second, the period of the Popular Front, working-class ethnic culture was seen as having an important political role. At the same time, Communist attitudes toward American culture changed: the view that U.S. culture was completely class-divided gave way to a recognition that some elements of the culture were shared by all classes. The Communist approach in this case was to emphasize the democratic currents prevalent in the culture, and Communists claimed the mantle of being the defenders of the democratic tradition. The shift to the Popular Front against Fascism in the mid-1930s also entailed a revision of previously held views of the family, toward which Communists had been very critical during the 1920s. Notwithstanding these theoretical changes, through the end of the 1940s Communist children's activities maintained their strong utopian flavor as Communists attempted to realize their social aspirations through to their next generation.

the soviet of children

The Young Pioneers of America and the Communist Children's Movement, 1922–1934

The Communist Children's Movement attempted to develop a children's political culture in which working-class consciousness and identification with the Communist movement would transcend ethnic or regional differences between children. They sought a culture that would provide an alternative to the conservatism of U.S. society in general. The movement emphasized the ability of youngsters to develop an autonomous political consciousness in order separate children from the socializing influences of bourgeois society. These influences, they held, included the working-class family as well as public schools, newspapers, churches, synagogues, and children's and youth organizations such as the Boy Scouts.

During the 1920s, the children's activities of the Socialist Party (SP) remained based in the Socialist Sunday schools organized before the First World War. However, by the mid-1930s the SP created a children's organization, the Red Falcons, modeled on European Social Democratic children's organizations; in part, this was to compete with the Communist children's organizations. In 1936, when the SP claimed to have fifty-four Falcon "Flights," they seemed to be strongest in the two regions where Socialists were strongest, New York and Milwaukee.[1] Unlike the Young Pioneers of the Communists, the Falcons did not organize children for political activity, but rather saw their task as educating children for political participation in the future.

The children's organizations of the Communist Party were semiautonomous sections of the Communist political movement. This meant, most importantly, that they were led by representatives of the Young Communist League (YCL) and the Communist Party, not by parents, and were the responsibility of the adult and youth political organization.

The first Communist children's organization was the junior section of the Young Workers League, the youth arm of the Workers Party. Between 1922 and 1925, the Workers Party was the legal, public face of a clandestine, "illegal" Communist Party. In 1926, after the Communist Party and the Young Communist League (YCL) became fully above-ground political organizations, the junior section of the Young Workers League became the Young Pioneers of America (YPA), the centerpiece of the Communist Children's Movement. Membership in the children's sections was intended to be broader than that in the party; it was to include working-class children whose parents were not Communists. The Pioneers were supposed to recruit these children in working-class neighborhoods and schools and train them to be future members of the YCL and the Communist Party. In reality, most Young Pioneers were children of Communist Party members and sympathizers.[2]

THE YOUNG PIONEERS OF AMERICA

The structure of the Young Pioneers mirrored that of the Communist Party. Local branches were organized on the basis of neighborhoods or schools, which were responsible to higher bodies organized at city and state level, which answered in turn to the National Pioneer Buro [sic]. Each level of leadership of the Young Pioneers included children and older members of the YCL, who had direct responsibility for the Young Pioneers. The Pioneers hoped that the neighborhood branches would become obsolete and be replaced by branches centered in schools. The school branches of the Young Pioneers were intended to be for children what the industrial cells of the Communist Party were for adults:

> At the formation of the Communist Children's Movement in the
> Capitalist countries, it was built up like the organizations of the Party
> and Youth, upon a territorial basis. . . .
> THIS CENTRAL AND COMMENCING POINT IS THE
> SCHOOL, WHICH IN MANY RESPECTS HAS A SIMILAR

IMPORTANCE FOR THE CHILDREN AS THE FACTORY HAS
FOR ADULT WORKERS.
     Here, in the school, they meet for the first time . . . an enemy world,
a part of the capitalist world. (caps. in original)[3]

Until 1926, the junior section of the Young Workers League published a magazine for children called the *Young Comrade*; it was then
renamed the *Young Pioneer*.[4] In 1931, the *Young Pioneer* changed its
name to the *New Pioneer,* which in 1934 became the publication of the
junior section of the International Workers Order.

In addition to developing their own groups, the Young Pioneers participated in the creation of the children's sections of organizations allied
with the Communist Party. In the early 1920s, the Juniors of the Young
Workers League organized the Famine Scout Clubs, affiliated with the
Communist-sponsored Russian Famine Relief efforts.[5] During the late
1920s and the early 1930s, organizations such as the Young Defenders
of the International Labor Defense, which campaigned to free the
Scottsboro Boys,[6] the International Worker's Order Juniors, the Nature
Friends Scouts, the Finnish Federation Pioneers, the Worker's Inter-
national Relief Scouts, the Unemployment Council Pioneers, and the
Junior Liberators were supported by the Young Pioneers of America
and were the constituent organizations of the Communist Children's
Movement.[7] Most of these organizations were represented at a 1934
"Children's Conference against War and Fascism." Children from the
children's section of the Russian National Mutual Aid Society, the
Jewish Schools (of the IWO), the Grand Street Settlement House, and
a Boy Scout troop were also represented.[8]

During strikes led organized by the Communist-led unions of the
Trade Union Educational League (TUEL) and, later, the Trade Union
Unity League (TUUL), the Young Pioneers created ad hoc organiza-
tions for the children of the strikers. In the Passaic textile strike of 1926,
the Gastonia textile strike of 1929, and during the strikes led by the
National Miners Union, children organized into strikers' children's
clubs engaged in fundraising, walked on picket lines, and were taught
Communist politics by Pioneer leaders.

Summer camps sponsored by the Young Pioneers, Workers International Relief (WIR), and Communist ethnic organizations were an integral part of the Pioneer program during the 1920s. These were perhaps

the most successful of the Communist children's programs and some lasted well into the 1950s. At the summer camps, the culture of the Communist movement and the Communist vision of political education for children could be realized in a context in which children were removed from the daily conservative influences of the larger society.

Pioneer troops generally met in Workers' Centers, Labor Lyceums, and halls owned by ethnic societies connected to the Communist Party. Troop leaders were members of the Young Communist League who had been specially selected to work with children. The meetings included discussions based on articles in the Pioneer magazines or of current events, a play activity or game, and planning for the political activities of the troop. If a troop was running properly, the children themselves were to initiate and lead the organization of the activities. Children would chair the meetings and record the minutes, and all troop officers were elected from among the Pioneers. The members of the YCL assigned to the Pioneer troop were to restrict themselves to facilitating the children's activities, not directing them.[9]

During the 1920s, the Young Pioneers engaged in a variety of political campaigns that were seen as being of particular concern to children, such as fighting injustices in school discipline and opposing militarist propaganda in schools. They called on their peers to stay out of school on May Day and fought for the racial integration of public recreational facilities and the unionization of child workers.

Because the Young Pioneers saw organizations like the Boy Scouts as the voice of the capitalists among working-class children, they sought to compete with them, presenting themselves as the revolutionary alternative.[10] A leaflet issued in a New York high school giving their overall ideology illustrated their views on the Boys Scouts:

> The Boy Scouts justify and glorify bosses' wars. They boast of the fact that Boy Scouts make the best soldiers and that Boy Scouts did service to the bosses in the last World War, which was only a war for the bosses' profit. . . .
>
> The Pioneers are against all bosses' wars. We say to the workers' children: Your real enemies are not the workers of any other country, but the bosses right here at home—the American capitalist class. . . .
>
> The Pioneers are fighting against the rotten conditions in the schools in working-class neighborhoods—against the fire traps, against the

overcrowding, against the part-time system. . . . We're fighting to spread the truth about the workers and bosses among the children and to win the workers' children for the working class.[11]

Another leaflet issued by the Young Pioneers in New York continued the analogy between children and workers as a means to organize children's political activity: "We must stick together with the workers on May 1. We must down our tools on May Day, our pencils, our pens, our books."[12]

In the midst of the Great Depression, the Pioneers sponsored a children's center on West 53rd Street in New York City under the auspices of WIR. At the center, opened in 1932, children from the predominantly Black neighborhood received free meals along with political education and recreational activities. Children were told about the Soviet Union and encouraged to march in May Day parades, as well as participating in demonstrations demanding that the schools provide shoes for the children of the unemployed.[13] The center was described by Preva Glusman and Morris Colman in an article in the WIR newspaper *Workers Life*:

> The Center has become a real Pioneer Center. New squads take turns each day cleaning up and helping with the other work. Afternoons there is a Pioneer arts and crafts circle, where the children paint, draw, sew bandannas, carve soap. An Indian boy has organized a bow and arrow team. A dance circle, football team, dramatic circle are being organized. The month of June will end up with a big show at which all the work of the children will be on exhibition. Every child treasures his copy of The New Pioneer.[14]

As adult Communist activists faced opposition from factory owners and, often, police, Pioneers likewise confronted hostility from school administrators and, often, police. In 1929, two students at Junior High School 61 in the Bronx were suspended from school for no reason other than being members of the Young Pioneers. In 1932, Black Pioneer Jimmy Ford was sentenced to one year in a children's reformatory for participating in a demonstration to allow Black children to swim in the Bronxdale Swimming Pool,[15] and Pioneer Rose Plotkin was arrested in a demonstration called in 1928 in solidarity with Nicaragua. After her arrest, she was held in the Home of the

Society for the Prevention of Cruelty to Children (SPCC), from where she wrote to the *Young Pioneer*, "Down with the SPCC—an agency of the bosses to jail workers' children."[16]

THE IDEAL OF CHILDREN'S AUTONOMY: THE CAREER OF HARRY EISMAN

The Pioneer ideal was centered around the autonomy of children from their families, an outlook based on the Communist views of the political capabilities of children (see chapter 2). They believed that children's loyalty to their families, based on the power of parents over children, tended to inculcate conservative values in children; this was true, they thought, regardless of the political sympathies of the parents. The Pioneers hoped to provide for children an alternative to the conservatism of family and ethnic ties by transferring their allegiance from their families to the Communist movement.

During the early 1930s, Harry Eisman was perhaps the best-known member of the Young Pioneers of America, and he was a hero in the Communist movement. Eisman's personal history, his role as a Pioneer leader, and the repression directed against him illustrated the Pioneer perspective that the autonomy of children was the road to revolutionary consciousness and that children's lives in the Communist movement could represent the socialist future—a break from the sordidness of capitalism.

Eisman was born in Kishenev, a city on the disputed border between Romania and Czarist Russia. He was orphaned when he was seven years of age, and at nine emigrated to the United States with his three older sisters. Two older brothers who were already in the United States sponsored their four younger siblings. One brother, who was doing well and had a family of his own, showed no inclination to take charge of the four children, and the other brother, a Communist housepainter who took them in, was too involved in the radical movement to pay much attention to the four children. So they began to live by themselves. Two of the sisters found work in the garment industry, and Harry and the youngest girl, Eda, went to school. Harry and Eda promptly joined the Young Pioneers, first in the Brownsville section of Brooklyn and later in the Bronx.[17] Having no parents and living independently, without adults, fit well into the Young Pioneer perspective that children's political and personal autonomy was a precondition for the development of revolutionary consciousness.

Eisman had been active in the Young Pioneers for five years when he was arrested at a "send-off" organized by the Young Pioneers at a dock where a delegation of Boy Scouts was boarding ship for the 1929 international Boy Scout Jamboree. He was convicted but paroled under the condition that he not participate in demonstrations. He then violated his parole by participating in the massive demonstration against unemployment in Union Square on 6 March 1930. For this offence, he faced six years in the "protective" care of the Home for Boys. At this point, the Young Pioneers of the Soviet Union invited him to live in the Soviet Union, an offer he accepted.

Eisman saw himself as a representative of a revolutionary generation of children. Writing of his early life, he explained:

> My American childhood was molded in the revolutionary movement. Joining the Pioneers in 1924, I have been steeped in the class struggle from the age of eleven. In 1926 I helped in the Passaic strike and I have marched on the picket lines with cloakmakers and furriers, cafeteria employees and fruit clerks in New York. I took part in nearly every workers' demonstration; I spoke often from the platform in the name of the Young Pioneers. These activities earned me the hatred of the capitalists and their servants in the public school system of New York. I was arrested seven times in strikes and demonstrations and suspended from school.[18]

Eisman's schools, JHS 61 and PS 89, both in the Bronx, were among the centers of Young Pioneer activity in New York. These were the schools attended by children who lived in the United Workers' Cooperative apartments on Allerton Avenue (mentioned in the introduction). The Coops, as they were called, were a block of apartments owned cooperatively by Communists and Communist sympathizers. In their own way, the Coops were an attempt at building socialism in one borough. As a center for the large Jewish Communist movement in the Bronx, the Coops sponsored a Pioneer troop and a YCL branch, as well as owning Camp Nitgedaigit, a resort in Beacon, New York.

A leaflet distributed in JHS 61 by the Pioneer branch during this period detailed the cases of three Young Pioneers punished for their

Pioneer activities—Bernard Kaplan, who was demoted, and Jeanette Rubin and Lebe Kaplan, who were kept back. For his part in Pioneer work, Eisman was transferred from JHS 61 to another school.[19]

The narrative of Eisman's life in the Young Pioneers, as written in his autobiographical pamphlet *An American Boy in the Soviet Union*, reflects two important aspects of the Communist perspective on the relationship between children and the revolutionary movement. During the first part of his life, Eisman was not subject to parental influence and thus was able to give his complete loyalty to the movement. As a reward for his activities as a Pioneer activist he was carried to the "future" in the Soviet Union, and he lived out his adult life there.[20]

INTERNATIONALIST IDENTITY AND THE PIONEERS' VIEW OF ETHNICITY

The Communist Party, wishing to be perceived as an American organization, deemphasized the largely immigrant character if its membership.[21] Similarly, the Young Pioneers presented themselves as an organization for all oppressed children, not only the children of immigrant Communists. In *Who Are the Young Pioneers?*, a pamphlet published in 1934, *New Pioneer* staff writer Martha Campion detailed the lives of Young Pioneer activists in what she claimed were true stories. Her examples included children of Pennsylvania miners, Southern Black sharecroppers, Midwestern farmers, a child millworker, and a newsboy. None of the children's ethnic backgrounds, except that of the African American child, were defined.[22]

The Pioneer magazines followed a similar pattern. There were numerous stories about Pioneer activity outside the United States; for example, in the Soviet Union, China, Japan, Germany, Cuba, and Nicaragua. Yet the only ethnic identifications given in stories about U.S. Young Pioneers were those of children with African American, American Indian, and Cuban backgrounds. Thus, in its analysis of ethnicity in the United States, the only distinction made by the Communist Party was that between members of European ethnic groups and members of racial or "national" minorities.

The activities of the Young Pioneers of America took place within this contradiction: that the base of the organization was among children of immigrants (children not yet assimilated into the mainstream culture of the United States, and indeed, resisting that assimilation), while, at the same time, the Pioneers wanted to be the means for spreading the Communist message to children from non-Communist, nonimmigrant backgrounds. In the 1920s, Young Pioneers in Brownsville, Brooklyn, were told that they had to conduct their meetings in English rather than Yiddish, even though some members of the troop spoke only Yiddish.[23] Another New York Pioneer troop was transferred, as a group, from their neighborhood in a Jewish community in Manhattan, to Brooklyn, and assigned to organize the non-Jewish children of longshoremen.[24]

The Communist emphasis on "internationalism," in which all forms of particular identity were counterposed against a universalist class consciousness, did not prevent the Young Pioneers from gaining their greatest strength in those areas where the adult Communist movement was characterized by ethnic, regional, and, sometimes, occupational features. The Young Pioneers reflected this intersection between ethnic and class consciousness within the revolutionary subcultures created by the Communist Party during the 1920s. The existence of these revolutionary subcultures did not necessarily correlate with political success, in traditional terms; rather, the creation of the Communist political culture occurred at those points where Communist social and political influence intersected with other political/cultural cleavages.

The Young Pioneers were strongest among children of immigrants, especially in the Eastern European Jewish and Finnish communities, which is also where the Communist Party received its greatest support. In greetings published in the *New Pioneer* during the early 1930s, most of the children's names seem to be of these two nationalities. The Jewish names predominate in the urban areas of New York, Chicago, Boston, and Los Angeles. The Finns were concentrated in Minnesota, Wisconsin, Ohio, Michigan, and Massachusetts.[25]

In New York City, the Young Pioneers were most active in the working-class Jewish sections of the Bronx and Brooklyn. The Pioneers' strongest section, as evidenced by the numbers of children absent from school on May Day in the late 1920s, was the area served by PS 89 and JHS 61 in the Bronx—the location of the Coops.[26] It is noteworthy that the Young Pioneers sometimes had branches organized on an ethnic basis, regardless of the official perspective of the organization to discourage this. In Minneapolis, an International Children's Day celebration was held in which the Pioneers of the Finnish Workers' Club and those of the Jewish Workers' Club presented a joint dramatic presentation, according to a report in the Finnish-language Communist newspaper *Työmies* for 6 November 1932.[27]

The ethnic basis of Young Pioneer organization could often be seen in the forms of activity undertaken in each area. For example, while Jewish Pioneers were often involved in the schools of the Workmen's Circle and later the Jewish People's Fraternal Order, Finnish Pioneer girls organized a Red Sewing Circle modeled on the socialist sewing circles that had been a fundamental activity of Finnish socialist women.[28]

Other ethnically oriented sections of the Pioneer movement included the Nature Friends Scouts—the children's section of the German-language left-wing hiking and nature organization, which engaged in extensive hiking, camping, and gymnastics modeled on the traditional German workers' *turnvereine* and hiking organizations[29]; all-Black Pioneer troops, reported in Charlotte, North Carolina, and Chattanooga, Tennessee[30]; and the Slovak Worker's Society, an ethnic fraternal benefit society organized before the First World War. The latter aimed to teach children "the Slovak language and . . . the spirit of Communism."[31] In 1932, the Slovak society organized a Pioneer troop in Newark, New Jersey.[32] Another ethnically oriented troop was one in New York City named for Julio Antonio Mella, the founder of the Cuban Communist Party.[33] Members of this troop were mostly Cuban Americans, as were the Pioneers in Tampa, Florida. Tampa Pioneer Vesper Romero became a Pioneer hero after being arrested for organizing children in support of a general strike called by Tampa cigar workers in 1931.[34]

THE YOUNG PIONEERS AS A JUNIOR COMMUNIST PARTY

The Young Pioneers were responsible for carrying out political work among children, as the Communist Party and the Young Communist League did among adults and youth. The belief that children were capable of political activity of their own, separate from their parents, led the Pioneers to focus on political, not exclusively educational, activities. The primary political activity of the Pioneers was routine branch activity: selling the Pioneer magazine, leafleting at schools, and attending demonstrations and celebrations sponsored by the Communist Party.

Perhaps the best illustration of the Young Pioneers' attempt to function as a junior Communist Party came in the late 1920s during Communist-led strikes. The Young Pioneers organized children's organizations among strikers children—a means of building support for the strikes among the workers' families as well as spreading the political message of the Young Pioneers among the children. In Passaic, New Jersey, during the massive Communist-led textile strike in 1926, Sophie Gerson, Miriam Silverfarb, and Martha Stone, all Young Pioneers or YCL leaders of the Pioneers, were sent to organize the strikers' children.

Children were often very aware of the issues of a strike. In the Passaic strike, children wrote to the strike bulletin of their own activities and responses to the strike. One child wrote:

> We strikers' children are getting sick and tired of the way Chief Zober has been treating the strikers. So we thought we would form a line and march to his house and let him look at the rags we were wearing and tell him to stop clubbing our parents. . . . So we marched along about 300 of us, and sang union songs. . . .
>
> The cops chased us, but every time we came to a corner, we formed a new picket line. Some of us got arrested, but the next day everybody was on the line again.[35]

Helen Z., a ten-year-old girl, wrote:

> I stand with rights, liberty, justice and humanity. I stand with strikers, and with labor unions, because they fight for right, liberty, justice and humanity. They fight for better working conditions, for better life and better world. . . .
>
> Who is against the strikers is against liberty, against justice, against humanity, against our right to live as people.[36]

At a Victory Playground built for children on a vacant lot in Passaic, Pioneer organizers discussed the issues of the strike with the children, read them stories from the *Young Pioneer*, and helped to organize games and plays.[37] Mary Heaton Vorse, the labor journalist, described the Victory Playground in her pamphlet on the Passaic strike:

Victory Playground was well equipped. There were showers for the kid-
dies, swings, see-saws and other amusements. Games and plays were
organized under the direction of experienced and capable leaders, who
donated their services for the summer. The carpentry and other work on
the grounds was all done by the strikers, and the cost of equipping the
playground was very small.

The playground was equipped with a children's kitchen and milk
station, and the children were given a nutritious meal and lots of milk
during the day. Women of the United Council of Workingclass
Housewives took care of the kitchen and the milk station.[38]

Children's strike activities were also reported during the New
Bedford, Massachusetts, textile strike of 1928, when 150 children participated in strikers' children's clubs.[39] Elizabeth Donnelly, a Boston
University drop-out, organized children's picket lines and held meetings at strike headquarters to explain the meaning of the strike to the
children. When she requested use of New Bedford playgrounds to
organize activities for strikers' children, the city turned her down.[40]
Similarly, as announced in the September 1931 issue of the *New Pioneer*,
a Textile Pioneer troop was organized in Putnam, Connecticut, during
a strike there.[41]

In the Gastonia, North Carolina strike of 1929, strikers' children
were organized into the Young Pioneers by Edith Saunders Miller, wife
of a New York Young Communist League leader.[42] Called to testify in
the case in which Fred Beal, her husband, and other Communist union
organizers were indicted for the murder of Gastonia Police Chief
Aderholt, she testified that during the strike she distributed copies of
the *Young Pioneer* at meetings of strikers' children and had tried to
teach the children to be loyal to the union.[43]

In nonimmigrant working-class communities, the Young Pioneers
were most successful where there was isolation from the mainstream of
American culture and a native tradition of political radicalism. In such
places, Communists were able to achieve cultural strength similar to
what they enjoyed in the Finnish and Jewish ethnic communities. In
mining communities during strikes led by the National Miners Union,
and in Plentywood, a small rural town in the northeastern part of
Montana, the Young Pioneers became, for a short period, the dominant
children's organization.

During the 1929 National Miners Union (NMU) strikes in the anthracite coal regions of Pennsylvania, the Young Pioneers sponsored Miners' Children's Clubs—clubs for striking miners' children. The purpose of the clubs was to educate children about the issues of the strike, to get the children to support their fathers in strike activity, and to collect money to support the strike. The children were also given lessons in Marxism and the activities of the Pioneers and the Communist Party.

The NMU, which led the strike, was organized in the futile effort made by miners to reform John L. Lewis's autocratic rule of the United Mine Workers of America (UMW). Communists were instrumental in this effort, and in fact it was they who led the breakaway NMU after the failure of the reform movement. The NMU was never a significant challenge to Lewis's union, but it was strong in areas where the UMW was very weak and the conditions for miners were particularly bad.

Ernest Rymer, a Pioneer leader from New York, was sent to Pennsylvania, during the summer of 1929, to help organize the children's clubs: a Finnish cooperative had given farmland to the clubs so that they could establish a children's camp. Rymer's first job was to confront the malnourishment and lack of clothing common among the miners' children. He said some of the children were so ill-fed and ill-clothed that he often had to put two children together in one bed so that they would be warm.[44]

The activities at the camp included classes on the Marxist analysis of American society, the ABCs of Communism, and recreational activities such as swimming and sports. Campers also supplied active strike support; one night, children from the Miners' Children's Club even swam across a river late at night to sneak into coal mine being worked by scabs and distribute leaflets to the miners.[45] Miners' Children's Club members also traveled to Pittsburgh to collect money to support the miners and their families during the strike.

Author Laura Gillfillan traveled to Pittsburgh with the children on one of their trips to raise money for strike support:

> The truck was crowded with a horde of ragged children, all singing at the top of their lungs. I caught the words:
>
> > "Wave, the banner,
> > Tri-UM-phant-lee!" . . .

I looked at the clothing of the . . . little girls. They were . . . dressed in finery infinitely more pitiful that my faded calico. . . .

These children, I thought, have dressed themselves in their best clothes to go begging.[46]

A miner's daughter described her impressions of that or a similar trip to Pittsburgh to collect money for the relief of the striking miners. In an article in the *New Pioneer*, she wrote:

We had such fun coming in to Pittsburgh. We sang and cheered and everything. People waved back at us and smiled. But when we got our boxes and pinned our green papers with the relief's seal on it that meant it was all right to give us money because it would be helping buy food for striking miners and their families (that's us) who go on picket lines to fight against starvation.

After a while the police took the boxes and the money away from the children and threatened to arrest them.[47]

The activities of the Miners' Children's Clubs were part of a radical political culture that developed in coal-mining communities during the late 1920s and early 1930s. This culture, in which a historic traditions of labor militancy became merged with the activities of the Communist Party, also gave birth to the miners' protest songs "Which Side Are You On?" and "I Don't Want Your Millions, Mister," which continue to be sung in the radical and labor movements.[48]

A similar pattern occurred in Sheridan County in the northeast corner of Montana. In the rural farming and mining areas outside the county seat of Plentywood, the Communist Party was the strongest political force during the late 1920s and early 1930s. It was based among populist-influenced farmers and Danish immigrants.[49] Under the auspices of the United Farmers' League, Communists were elected to the posts of sheriff and other county offices, and the local newspaper, *The Producers News*, edited by Charles "Red Flag" Taylor, while continuing to cover local matters, also presented the Communist viewpoint on international and national events.[50] Branches of the Young Communist League and Young Pioneers met at the Farmer-Labor Temple in Plentywood, the center of the town's Communist social and political activities.[51]

Janice Salisbury, the daughter of Rodney Salisbury, the sheriff and leader of the Montana United Farmers' League, was a leader of the Young Pioneers in Sheridan County and when she died during an emergency appendectomy in 1932, she was given a funeral filled with Communist ritual and ceremony. The *Producer's News* reported on her funeral:

> Many farmers and townspeople were forced to stand in the Farmer-Labor Temple which was crowded to capacity when the funeral started at half past two. The coffin was accompanied from the entrance to the front of the hall by the Young Pioneers, led by two Pioneers bearing a Red Flag. When the coffin had been placed in the front of the hall, the Pioneers arranged the flowers that had been sent by the Young Pioneers, her school mates, the United Farmers League, the Producers News and the Communist Party, and others. The windows and the stage were covered with red and Black drapings, decorated with hammer and sickle emblems. Over the flowers on the coffin the Pioneers draped the Red Flag.[52]

THE SOVIET OF CHILDREN: THE YOUNG PIONEER SUMMER CAMPS

The most popular activities of the Communist children's movement were the Pioneer summer camps. These camps were the events most likely to reach beyond the children of Communists themselves. The organizing of children was effective during strikes, but there was often little holdover when the strikes ended. The summer camps, which became a central feature of Communist children's activities during the 1930s and 1940s, not only offered outdoor recreation to children who could not ordinarily afford it, but provided an institutional setting where a Communist political culture could be developed away from the hostility of the larger society, as mentioned earlier.

Most of the children's camps organized during the 1920s were open for only part of the year,[53] operating for from two to six weeks during the summer on land that was borrowed or rented from political sympathizers. These camps were sponsored by the Young Pioneers, the WIR (the Communist strike-support organization), and ethnic, left-wing fraternal societies. The makeup of the sponsoring groups differed from locality to locality, depending on the what groups were in the local Communist Party's sphere of influence. For example, in 1929 the groups organizing the Workers' Children's Camp near Los Angeles included the Young Pioneers, the Non-Partisan Jewish Workers' Schools, the Miners' Relief Scouts, Friends of Culture, and the Finnish, Ukrainian, and Czech Labor Schools.[54]

In 1928, the *Young Comrade*, a New York publication of the Young Pioneers, reported Pioneer camps in Chicago, Grand Rapids, Michigan, Boston, and Philadelphia; there were also WIR camps in New Jersey and New York.[55] The *Työmies*, the Finnish-language Communist daily, reported plans for seventeen WIR camps in the centers of Finnish population in north-central states in 1930.[56] Anti-Communist writer Elizabeth Dilling claimed that, by 1930, "in New York State alone over 15,000 young Communists are turned out each year from these camps."[57] Even allowing for some exaggeration on Dilling's part, this shows a substantial network of children's camps operated by Communists by the end of the 1920s.

The purpose of the Pioneer camps was reported by Rose Pastor Stokes in an article in *Solidarity*. Writing about WIR camps held in 1929, she said a camp near San Francisco aimed to "give the worker's child a summer vacation, an understanding of workers solidarity, co-operation and collective work, as well as acquaint the child with the conditions and organization of the workers, thereby increasing the knowledge and sympathy with and for, the interests of the working class."[58]

The camps were generally able to house between 25 and 30 children, although a camp in Wisconsin once reported an attendance of 125 children.[59] Most of the children came from families within the orbit of the Communist Party. Sessions at the camps lasted for one or two weeks. The cost of a stay was kept low, ranging from 25 cents a day at Workers Park in the Minnesota Iron Range[60] to $6 a week at the camp near Los Angeles.[61]

The structure of camp governance attempted to create a living model of socialism for both the children and the adults in the camp. Patterned on the Soviet political structure—indeed, in many camps, the assembly of child and adult representatives was known as the camp soviet—the structure reflected Communist views on the relationship between children and adults.

The children were organized into squads, or collectives, that for the time camp was in session were supposed to function as political units. Squads at the camp at Iron River, Wisconsin, in 1932 were named Lenin, Octobrists, Tom Mooney, Red Sparks, Marx, and Stalin.[62] Children were expected to elect from among themselves members of committees that would guide the work of the camp. At the camp near Los Angeles, children elected squad captains, an agitprop director, a literary agent, a social director, a sanitation director, and a sports director.[63] There was often an additional structure of adults—parents, camp staff, and members of the organizations sponsoring the camp—to supervise the activities of the children; however, in addition to there being committees made up solely of children, child representatives sat on all the adult committees.[64]

In the vision of socialism expressed in the Pioneer summer camps, children occupied the role of the proletariat; adults were in the role of the party. In the Communist view, children, like the proletariat under socialism, needed guidance coupled with autonomy and power.

Daily life at the camps was organized to express this perspective, which the Communists hoped would be carried over into political life after the camp. Pioneer Walter Stenroos described camp life in a letter to the *New Pioneer*: "I was on a vacation at the Pioneer Camp in Santa Cruz, California. First thing in the morning we had the Pioneer pledge, then we had exercises, breakfast, and cleaned out our tents and made the beds. We had classes after that—arts and crafts, journalism and dramatics. Then swimming games and after lunch story hour and more games. After supper there was a bonfire, dance or short hike. Then we went to bed."[65]

The pledge Stenroos referred to was the early-morning salute to the Red Flag —a ceremony that was nearly universal at the Pioneer camps. In words that can be seen in contrast to the patriotic Pledge of Allegiance, the Pioneer salute said:

> I pledge allegiance to the worker's flag and to the cause for which it stands, one aim throughout our lives, freedom for the working class.[66]

That aspect of the Communist movement that tended to make of the movement a world unto itself reached its highest expression in the Pioneer summer camps. Everything about the life at the camps was directed toward the end of creating an identification between the children and the Communist movement: The stories read at story hour came from the Pioneer magazines or from collections of children's stories published by the Communist Party; they included Herminia zur Muhlen's *Fairy Tales for Worker's Children*, *Science and History for Boys and Girls* by William Montgomery Brown, and Martha Campion's *Who Are the Young Pioneers?*[67] Many of the songs the children sang came from the *Pioneer Song Book*, with words such as

> *1–2–3 pioneers are we,*
> *We're fighting for the working class,*
> *Against the bourgeoisie.*

Another song proclaimed:

> *We're marching towards the morning,*
> *We're struggling comrades all.*
> *Our aims are set on victory,*
> *Our enemies must fall.*
> *With ordered step, red flag unfurled,*
> *We'll make a new and better world.*
> *We are the youthful guardsmen of the*
> *proletariat.*[68]

Programs to connect the activities of the children in the summer camps to the larger movement took many forms. All camps had study groups and classes to "teach the children the condition of the workers and their children" and to "develop in the child an understanding of the need for organization and to actively take part in their own struggles, as well as help in the struggles of the workers in general."[69] Special efforts were made to bring to the camps children who were from outside the particular base of the camp. Thus the Philadelphia WIR invited African American Boy Scouts who had been excluded from the Boy Scout camps. Children of the strikers at Gastonia, North Carolina, spent the summer at camps in Philadelphia and New York.[70]

The organization of the camps showed that the Communists believed that children would be more likely to absorb their political/cultural message where it informed the total camp experience—but this did not mean that all activities took place in an insular setting. For example, the children at the Miners' Children's Club camp participated not just in camp cultural activities but also in strike support, and

children at a Pioneer camp in Wisconsin took a petition to free the
Scottsboro defendants to a nearby "reformist" Co-operative Camp.[71]
Children at other camps collected money for Miners' Relief and to support other striking workers. Such excursions were, however, a minor
part of the camp program, which ultimately remained focused on the
development of internal camp life.

The Young Pioneer movement and the camps associated with it centered their efforts on building a culture of Communism that was set off
from both the ethnic roots of so many of the children and the larger U.S.
culture in which these children were growing up. This attempt to create a separate culture was never entirely successful, even among supporters of the Communist political program. The strength of the ethnic
organizations and the desires of radical parents that the children's programs teach an ethnic, as well as political, identification led to conflicts
between the parents and the party.

In an article entitled "Work This Summer among the Workers'
Children," Lily Beck wrote:

> There is still the old tendency in some communities to have summer
> schools for the sole purpose of teaching the children reading and writing
> in Finnish. One of our comrades instructing at a small community hav-
> ing a class of 40 asked the class this question:
>
> "Why have you come to Summer School?" One little boy replies: "To
> learn to read and write Finn."
>
> "And for anything else?"
>
> Another little comrade answered–"I know, to learn about the work-
> ing class and the Young Pioneers, too!"
>
> From this we see that our children's Summer camps to the present
> have not been what they should have been. . . . The Pioneer organization
> is not a Finnish club in a community. It is an international organization
> of proletarian children.[72]

Communists faced a tension in the relationship between the
Communist political culture and that of American culture in general. As
revolutionaries, Communists were opposed to much in American culture, seeing it only as the ideological expression of capitalist domination.
For immigrant radicals, this alienation was heightened by the cultural
alienation they experienced through not knowing the language and
often being excluded from full participation in the society. Yet the

Communists' professed goal of social transformation required them to engage in activities aimed at having an impact on American society. Thus they tried to get the children's organizations to involve children in outwardly directed political activities. At the same time, the organizations and the summer camps were designed to provide a more self-contained experience. The contradictions between these two purposes in the activities of the children's movement were never fully resolved.

On one level, Communists hoped that by encouraging the use of English among Pioneers, these children would grow up with roots in the United States, rather than Europe. To recruit more children of native-born parents, Pioneer leaders tried to provide activities more in tune with what American children were interested in. For example, the Labor Sports Union and Pioneer athletic clubs sponsored tournaments in track, swimming, and baseball, wishing to place these familiar sports in a radical context.[73]

The high point in the development of the Young Pioneer movement occurred after the onset of the Great Depression. The Communist Party, with its confrontation of the ensuing massive poverty and social upheaval, grew in influence and size; at the same time, the children's activities of the party became more focused. Pioneers, campaigning for free meals and clothing for the children of the unemployed, publicized instances of malnutrition and disease among poor children.

In the beginning, the structure of these activities remained much as they had been throughout the 1920s. The Communist Party was in the middle of its "sectarian" third period and the vehemence of its attacks on liberals, reformers, and Socialists rivaled that of its attacks on capitalism. By 1934, however, the Communist-oriented children's activities began to change, developing the character they would have during the rest of the 1930s and into the 1940s. In particular, these activities after 1934 were oriented much more toward finding an accommodation between the movement culture of the Communist Party and both the ethnic cultures of the immigrants and that of the United States in general. These changes coincided with the general shift in Communist strategy to what was characterized as the Popular Front against Fascism. This policy was instituted in 1936, but changes in the children's activities tending in this direction began earlier.

Regardless of whether the shift in the political direction of the Communist Party came from abroad or was in response to internal developments within the U.S. Communist movement, the alterations in children's activities reflected an attempt to resolve problems that had been endemic to the Pioneers since the early 1920s. The switch in overall political strategy allowed the development of children's programs in which the relationship between children and their immigrant parents, and between Communists' children and American culture, became the central concern.

The Young Pioneers of America was dissolved in 1934. The political perspective it had evolved since the early 1920s no longer reflected the concerns either of the Communist Party or of Communist parents. The Communist Party by this time was looking to influence organizations with greater appeal outside its own ranks, rather than to support a multiplicity of organizations whose politics mirrored those of the CP itself. At the same time, the constituency for Communist children's activities was interested in a different form of children's organization than what was offered by the Young Pioneers. After 1934, the junior section of the International Workers Order, which had first been organized in 1930 when the IWO itself was first organized, became the primary organization for Communist children's activities. In the IWO Juniors, the relationship between children and their parents, particularly with regard to their outlook on ethnicity, expressed the desires of Communist parents more than had been the case with the Young Pioneers.

"americans all! immigrants all!"

Children of the Popular Front, 1934–1945

During the 1920s and early 1930s, the Communist Party rejected both the ethnic/cultural particularities of working-class immigrants and the national culture and politics of the United States. The Communists perceived the ethnic cultures of immigrant workers as a divisive force that limited the ability of the working class to unite politically. In particular, the Communists hoped that immigrant workers would learn English and give up the religious and cultural distinctiveness that separated them from "American" workers. At the same time, they believed that the national political culture of the United States reflected the interests of the capitalist ruling class. The Communist alternative was a "proletarian" outlook based in Marxism and expressed as a universalist internationalism that was counterposed against both the parochialism of ethnic cultures and the bourgeois nationalist politics of the dominant culture. The Communists hoped that the development of this "proletarian" perspective would provide a means for both Americanizing the party and for grounding itself in the U.S. working class.

Ironically, American Communists achieved their greatest influence during the 1930s and 1940s, when they abandoned this position and came not only to accept and celebrate the ethnic cultures of immigrant workers but to begin to define a "democratic" and "progressive" strand in the political traditions of the United States with which they could identify. This was expressed in the Communist slogan of the late 1930s, "Communism is Twentieth-Century Americanism."

From 1936 to 1945, the Communist Party grew into the largest left-wing force in U.S. society since the decline of the Socialist Party. The CP helped to organize unions in mass-production industries as part of the Congress of Industrial Organizations (CIO), and came to lead many of them. Communist influence among intellectuals and other sections of the middle class also grew, and Communism achieved, for a time, a kind of respectability in American life. This change in fortune grew from the party's earlier efforts during the 1920s and early 1930s, as well as from changes in the strategy of the Comintern after the Seventh Comintern Congress of 1935.

The strategy of the United and Popular Fronts against Fascism as articulated by the Communist International after 1935 called for alliances between Communists and non-Communist sectors of the working-class movement and between Communists and the "progressive" sectors of the middle and, even, the upper classes.[1]

Historical analyses that view the development of CP policy as only responsive to directives from the Comintern have tended to date this change in outlook from the mid-1930s; however, in the arena where American Communist political culture was being generated, the change in emphasis is evident earlier in the 1930s.

During the 1930s and 1940s, the International Workers Order (IWO), a federation of ethnic fraternal benefit societies, was the largest of the Communist-led mass organizations. After the Young Pioneers of America dissolved in 1934, its role as the primary children's organization of the Communist movement was taken over by its children's section, the IWO Juniors. The IWO had been organized by Communists who had split from the Jewish socialist Workmen's Circle (WC) in 1930. After organizing the Jewish People's Fraternal Order (JPFO) to compete with the WC, the Communists decided to create a fraternal society that would also encompass other ethnic organizations.[2]

The creation of the IWO in 1930 was the result of long-term divisions between the "Left" (Communists) and the "Right" (Socialists) within the Jewish socialist Workmen's Circle. The struggle for control of the organization had been sharp throughout the 1920s, and in 1929 the Communists finally left the WC and formed the Jewish People's Fraternal Order (JPFO). This would become the initiator and centerpiece of the IWO.[3] In fact, the final division between Communists and Socialists in the Workmen's Circle had been anticipated in 1926 when

Communists and Communist sympathizers active in the children's schools left the organization to begin the Non-Partisan Jewish Workers Schools. In New York, seventeen of twenty-four schools became part of the new organization.[4]

The IWO united the JPFO with the other ethnic fraternal societies whose leadership was associated with the Communist Party. Initially, the IWO united the Jewish People's Fraternal Order with the Hungarian Workmen's Sick, Benevolent and Educational Federation and the Slovak Workers Society. Later, in 1935, the Russian National Mutual Aid Society affiliated, and in 1941 the Finnish American Mutual Aid Society, a descendent of the Finnish Socialist Federation and Finnish Workers' Federation, joined. Once the IWO model of a federation of ethnically organized fraternal societies was established, the order set about creating ethnic societies among groups without a significant Communist-led ethnic association. Sections affiliated to the IWO were organized among Italians, Poles, Ukrainians, Rumanians, Croatians, Greeks, Czechs, and others.[5] The Cervantes Fraternal Society, organized for Spanish-speaking immigrants, had sections for Spaniards, Cubans, Puerto Ricans, and Mexicans; later, there were English-speaking sections, some with predominantly African American membership.[6]

The main function of the International Workers Order was to continue the mutual-benefit functions of the ethnic societies by providing low-cost insurance to working-class families. In addition, the IWO assumed the task of organizing the cultural life of Communist-oriented immigrants and their families. Because the IWO was a federation, composed of autonomous fraternal organizations, it became a principal organization for Communists and sympathizers whose strongest allegiance was to their ethnic communities.

The ethnic fraternal societies achieved greater importance after the "bolshevization" of the Communist Party—a process completed by 1929. One of the central features of "bolshevization" in the United States was that the foreign-language federations, which had been constituent elements of the party, were disbanded. These federations had developed from their Socialist Party predecessors and had been crucial to the creation of the Communist Party. Communists who had been members of foreign-language federations were supposed to join Communist Party branches based in factories and neighborhoods. The leadership of the Communist Party hoped that this would set the stage for the "Americanization" of the party.

Many Communists did not share the views of the CP leadership that ethnic identification contradicted revolutionary politics. They resisted the transition from the foreign-language federations to the "international" industrial or geographic units, and this aspect of "Bolshevization" weakened the CP among some of its most important supporters. For example, among Finnish-American Communists, who had been members of the Finnish Federation of the Workers Party, only about one-third of the federation's members joined the new organizations of the party.[7] Indeed, the Finnish Workers Federation, the Communist-oriented successor to the Finnish Socialist Federation and the Finnish Federation of the Workers Party, jealously guarded its autonomy and did not join the International Workers Order until 1941.[8] After the abolition of the foreign-language federations, the main voice of the Communist Party within the immigrant communities was that of the fraternal benefit societies, most of whom became part of the IWO. Some of these societies, such as the Workmen's Circle, split between Communists and Socialists during the 1920s; others, such as the Slovak Workers Society, changed their allegiance from the Socialist to the Communist Party without suffering division.

During the early 1930s, the leaders of the IWO looked forward to the organization's eventual obsolescence. Under socialism, they believed, the state would provide for health care and old-age security, making IWO-style mutual aid unnecessary. Furthermore, the division of the working class into diverse ethnic groups, each speaking its own language, would change as soon as immigrants had fully assimilated into American life.[9]

Over the course of the 1930s and 1940s, the IWO developed a perspective that, at one and the same time, reflected the Marxism of the Communist Party and yet diverged from it. They called it Labor Fraternalism. This view united the IWO's emphasis on mutual aid with a recognition of the cultural diversity of the U.S. working class.[10] Radicals could, according to the IWO, become the catalyst for progressive social change by responding to the immediate, daily, cultural and economic needs of the working class. The various ethnic communities would be united in a pluralist federation, politically identified with the universalist Marxist political movement, led by the Communist Party.

The CP, in fact, provided the overall political stance and much of the leadership for the IWO. The IWO became the center of the political culture of Popular Front Communism in working-class communities. Through its educational and cultural activities, the IWO made Communism attractive to working-class immigrants and their children, and the IWO membership was a base of support for the CP's political activities. For example, when Communist organizers for the Steel Workers Organizing Committee went to Pittsburgh during the mid-1930s, their first contacts among the steelworkers were members of IWO fraternal lodges.[11]

Because the IWO saw itself as serving the immediate cultural and social needs of its working-class constituents, it was far more attuned than the Communist Party had been to the concerns of radical parents with the education and socialization of their children. The roots of the IWO in established fraternal societies and, in particular, the Workmen's Circle, meant that alternative radical ethnic educational institutions were in many cases already established when the order was founded.

Most of the programs organized for children by the Communist movement in the 1930s and 1940s were under the auspices of the International Workers Order. Through its after-school programs, its children's organization (the IWO Juniors), and summer camps, the IWO created a network of activities to help radical parents pass on their ethnic and political culture to their children. Although the insurance and mutual-aid aspects of the organization were, perhaps, the overt raison d'être of the IWO and its constituent organizations, the children's programs formed the center of its role in the creation of a radical cultural milieu.

In addition to revising the perspective on ethnicity that had been part of Communist children's activities during the period of the Young Pioneers, the IWO also made new approaches to the issue of the proletarian family. Out went the metaphor of the family as a representation of class struggle—parents vs. children; in the new view, divisions within the working-class family were a metaphor for divisions within the working class as a whole. Describing the goals of the IWO's children's programs in 1938, Jerry Trauber, the order's national junior director, said: "Our education aims at creating the same unity and harmony within the working-class family that should exist within the working class as a whole."[12] Max Bedacht, an IWO leader for many years, writing of the role of the IWO Juniors in his pamphlet *Labor Fraternalism,* echoed Trauber's position:

> Social enlightenment does not fall into the laps of the citizens from the skies. It must be generated in progressive homes and organizations. . . . The International Workers Order must convince its members that failure to raise their children into socially conscious and actively progressive citizens might prove fatal to our liberties. . . .
>
> The need of generating a social conscience in the coming generation requires the expansion of comradeship between individual parents and their children into the comradeship of all working men and women, with the masses of their children.[13]

The junior section of the IWO, founded in 1933,[14] initially bore the same relation to the Young Pioneers as did the IWO to the Communist Party: it provided for children what the IWO did for adults, including special insurance for children as well as cultural and educational activities. The Juniors were a success. By 1940, the section had almost twenty thousand members.[15] Between 1930 and 1934, the Juniors were part of the Communist Children's Movement that centered around the Young Pioneers. This movement included such organizations as the children's section of the Russian National Mutual Aid Society, the Nature Friends Scouts, the Finnish Federation Pioneers, and the Young Defenders of the International Labor Defense.[16]

Jerry Trauber described how the potential constituency for the IWO Juniors was much larger than had been that for the Young Pioneers: "The possibilities for children's work in the IWO are tremendous. In the first place, because of the worker's interest in insuring his child. Secondly, because the Order is a mass organization which by its insurance feature reaches thousands of workers not reached by other working-class organizations."[17]

Trauber argued that the Juniors should be a catalyst for the development of revolutionary consciousness among children from non-Communist families: "Another problem which the Junior section faces is that of working among children organized by the various capitalist led fraternal organizations. For example, all sorts of Knights, Elks, Moose, church orders, brotherhood unions, language orders, organize children's groups. . . . Around 20,000,000 workers in the U.S. belong to fraternal organizations led by the bosses and hundreds of thousands of children are under their influence."[18]

The fundamental difference between the IWO Juniors and the Young Pioneers was that the Juniors were based in the adult lodges of the IWO, whereas the Pioneers were organized in neighborhoods and public schools. Indeed, Trauber argued in the article cited above that the term for the adult organization with which the junior branch was associated be changed from "sponsoring" organization to "parent" organization, to emphasize the idea that the relations between the Juniors and the adults of the order were supposed to replicate, rather than replace, the relations between parents and children.[19]

The goal of the IWO was to have the Juniors be an organization where a new relationship between immigrant Communist parents and their English-speaking children could be developed—one in which the ideals of the parents could be translated into an American context. Max Bedacht, general secretary of the IWO during this period, wrote in the mid-1930s that "every organizer and leader of the order must therefore see the need of providing a field where the children can work and learn and be active together with their parents, for the same objectives as their parents and in the spirit of their parents."[20]

These efforts were not only for the benefit of the children. It was thought that having a strong children's organization would strengthen the adult lodges as well. A member of the IWO Juniors from Ohio wrote in 1936: "The Juniors are also a great help to the adult branches. Through experience we see that before our Juniors were organized hardly anyone showed up at meetings. But now, over three-fourths of the adults attend the meetings."[21]

The children in the IWO Juniors were not simply on the receiving end of the process of ethnic cultural preservation. Over the course of the 1930s and 1940s, the Juniors became engaged in a process whereby ethnic identities were constructed in line with the vision of the IWO. A pamphlet for directors of Junior lodges published in 1946 expressed it this way:

> While it is educationally desirable that the child should grow up with a particular appreciation of the culture and democratic traditions of his own people and of the land of their origin—it is also imperative to avoid sectarian, insular, and nationalistic development. Our children are growing up as Americans. Their language is English. The purpose of developing their understanding of their own national background is to promote their integration into American life on a *higher, more socially conscious plane.* (italics in original)[22]

Meetings of the IWO Juniors included presentations and projects based on the history and culture of the sponsoring ethnic group. Many Junior branches were associated with schools where the language of the immigrant's home country was taught. Some, such as the Ukrainian, Russian, and Carpatho-Russian branches, developed specialized programs in folkdancing. In all of these activities there was the attempt to provide a "proletarian" or, later, "progressive" framework. Thus the Italian lodges learned about Garibaldi, the Hungarians, about Kossuth, and the Latin American branches learned about the Puerto Rican Betances and the Cuban José Martí.

A booklet issued by the educational department of the Juniors illustrates the "progressive" interpretation of Hungarian history in a form intended for children. Entitled *The Hungarian People: Their Traditions and Contributions,* it proclaimed: "The Hungarian people have a rich background of struggle and national achievement. Time and again they have risen up to free their nation from the iron heel of foreign domination, to release the peasantry from exploiting landlords. From their ranks have emerged heroes, mighty as those heroes who made their mark in history at Lexington and Gettysburg, fighting for independence and democracy."[23] The booklet goes on to describe the history of Hungary, concentrating on the struggle for independence from the Austrian Empire and including coverage of a medieval peasant revolt and the short-lived Soviet government of 1918–19. The booklet also contained recipes for traditional Hungarian foods, descriptions of folk dances, and short biographies of prominent, non-Communist Americans of Hungarian descent such as Eugene Ormandy, Harry Houdini, and Joseph Pulitzer.[24]

It is interesting to note that there is neither revolutionary rhetoric nor even mention of socialism in the pamphlet. The revolutionary government of Hungary at the end of the First World War is referred to as a "real people's government" whose establishment was contributed to by "a large and powerful trade union movement."[25] This subordination of revolutionary politics to ethnicity was characteristic of the IWO in the late 1930s, and even more so during the 1940s. Immigrant radicals attempted to create a space within American culture for themselves by identifying a national and ethnic history that articulated with the Popular Front perspective on American democracy of the Communist Party during that period.

By emphasizing a new form of ethnic identity, the IWO Juniors created a social space for the children of immigrant radicals that was neither committed to preserving an intact culture nor uncritically assimilationist toward the culture of the United States. While the links between the junior organizations and the adult lodges maintained the ethnic character of the IWO, the incorporation of American culture into the activities of the Juniors allowed both parents and children a structured setting in which they could negotiate their relationship with the dominant culture. The Juniors openly borrowed "American" recreational and educational programs from mainstream children's organizations like the YMCAs and the Boy Scouts. In *Trips and Outings for Juniors,* the authors state: "The best reference for hiking, camping out, etc., is the boy scout handbook. This is an excellent, scientific work on the subject and should be consulted by any group leader who wants to conduct any form of hike, camping, or camp craft.[26]

The Juniors also sponsored sports teams in basketball and baseball that competed in IWO leagues. These were an outgrowth of the Labor Sports Union and Communist Youth athletic clubs of the earlier period, but unlike their predecessors they also competed against teams from other amateur sports organizations. The *New Order* monthly magazine of the IWO played up these sports activities to show how integrated the children of IWO members had become in American life. In addition, the solidarity among different ethnic groups could be illustrated by the friendly competition on the basketball court between, say, a Slovak and a Hungarian team, or, more importantly, when an Eastern European IWO team would play a team from a Black organization.

Sports came to represent the openness of the IWO to "American" culture and a rejection of ethnic insularity. One IWO writer criticized IWO practice in this area as "shoddy" and argued for increased attention to sports as a way of reaching American workers and "Americanizing" the IWO:

One of the most important phases of American life is Sports. It is necessary for us to pay special attention to this field of activity, especially when we face the task of Americanizing the Order. . . .

The standards of the average American in sports is very high and his respect can not be won by approaching the problem in a shoddy manner. The "shoddy manner" can be described as the approach that many of our

Youth and adult branches have had in the past. . . . The branch approaches the whole matter hesitantly and in a sectarian manner. At best its attempt at sports here is a concession to the propaganda and demand for more American activities in our Order.[27]

Thus at the opening of the IWO softball tournament in 1938, New York Yankee baseball hero Joe Dimaggio threw out the first ball.[28]

Another important activity of the Juniors in the late 1930s was the drum-and-bugle corps and marching bands. At national conventions of the IWO Junior marching bands led the parades, and at IWO Day at the 1939 New York World's Fair, Junior matching bands played all day. The first Junior marching band was organized in Chicago in 1933,[29] and by 1938 there were fifty-five Junior marching bands throughout the country.[30] It is difficult to discern why these bands were so important in the Junior program, other than it was for the same reasons these bands are popular among schools and mainstream fraternal organizations: the instruments can be learned quickly; the music is meant to be marched to; and the activities associated with marching bands such as travel and performing appeal to young people.

Other activities sponsored by the Juniors included art classes, music lessons, and dance classes. What these activities indicate is that the IWO was paying increased attention the personal and cultural development of the children in ways that were more compatible with mainstream American culture. By the end of the 1930s, this emphasis marks the crucial difference between the IWO Juniors and the Young Pioneers, for whom the political and ideological development of children was most important.

There were two intertwining trajectories in the ongoing relationship between the radical political culture developed by the International Workers Order during the late 1930s and the politics of the Communist Party. The IWO projected a vision of socialism, organizationally based in ethnic communities and tied to the larger political world through the Communist Party. In this context, the activities of IWO Juniors were directed toward synthesizing an American radicalism from the traditions of the non-English-speaking parents and the culture in which the American-born children of immigrants were growing up.

The IWO project of transmitting and constructing a radical political culture among the working-class immigrants and their children contained within it a contradictory element. This emerged in the late 1930s and flowered during the Second World War. The IWO began to move away from clear advocacy of socialism as a solution to workers' problems, and began to project the activities of the order as an alternative American way of life.

For both the Communist Party and the IWO, the campaign to organize the CIO unions during the latter half of the 1930s and their support for the U.S. effort in the Second World War facilitated this process. As the activities of the IWO came to focus on issues that aligned them with Americans far outside the orbit of the CP, the members of the order came to claim a place inside U.S. society as an alternative to revolutionary isolation. The question became whether the educational and cultural goals of the IWO were to make better radicals or better Americans.

Communists were in the forefront of the upsurge in trade union organization spearheaded by the CIO. Rank-and-file Communists helped to initiate many of the new industrial unions, and the Communist Party actively supported the new CIO unions. IWO members actively participated in these efforts as well, and the order began to refer to itself as "Labor's Fraternal Organization." Junior activities, likewise, encouraged children's identification with the labor movement as well as with ethnic communities. By the late 1930s and early 1940s, the rhetoric of class struggle and socialist revolution were gone from IWO discussions of the role of children's organization, to be replaced by the rhetoric of the "labor and progressive" movements. As Jerry Trauber wrote in 1938: "One of the greatest contributions that our Order can make to the progressive and labor movements of this country is the establishment of a wide network of Junior lodges which carry the inspiration and ideals of these movements to the younger generation."[31]

In fact, the connection between the IWO and the labor movement did open avenues for growth in the IWO as a whole, and for the Juniors in particular. For example, the IWO children's camp near Cleveland, Ohio, Camp Robin Hood, was sponsored both by IWO-affiliated organizations and trade unions. Junior branches in Pennsylvania and New York were jointly sponsored by an IWO lodge and a trade union local.[32] In Chicago, during the Little Steel Strike of 1937, IWO Junior branches organized a massive all-children's picket line, and Junior marching bands played at the victory celebration at the end of the strike.[33]

Illustrative of the changes that occurred in children's work in the
IWO during this period was a conference sponsored by the junior section in 1941 on "Labor's Children in a World at War." The conference
was held after the German invasion of the Soviet Union and the conse-
quent change in the CP's antiwar stance that they held during the period
of the Nazi-Soviet pact. The purpose of the conference was to discuss the
effects of U.S. participation in the war on children, and to plan ways to
involve children in the war effort. The conference included representatives of the Polish, Jewish, Hungarian, and Slovak sections of the IWO
from across the country, as well as representatives from the Cleveland
Industrial Council of the CIO, the CIO Women's Auxiliaries, the all-
Black International Benevolent Protective Order of Elks, and the
Teachers, Furriers, Shoe Workers, and Retail Workers unions.[34]

Max Bedacht, general secretary of the IWO, argued that efforts to
transmit radical social values to children had to be stepped up. He kept
the radical political goals of the IWO's founders in the forefront when
he spoke at the conference. Bedacht warned that even in the new circumstances caused by the war, concerted efforts had to be made to bring
children to what he called "social consciousness":

> They [children] need as much and even more guidance and loving care
> for their first steps into social consciousness as they need and get for their
> first physical steps. . . . The tremendously important guidance of the chil-
> dren by experience can only be brought to them by the cooperative
> efforts of working people. To supply that guidance the children must be
> made integral parts of the social world of their parents. They must be
> initiated into the work and functioning of the organizations of their par-
> ents. They must be supplied the atmosphere and air of the common aspi-
> rations of their parents.[35]

However, by this time Bedacht was a minority voice within the IWO.
By 1947, he had resigned his position in the IWO and one year later was
expelled from the Communist Party.[36] Ernest Rymer, former national
director of the Young Pioneers, had returned to work in children's
organizations and had replaced Jerry Trauber as the national director
of the Juniors. In his opening remarks, Rymer expressed the aims for
the conference in terms that illustrate the efforts of the IWO Juniors to
join the mainstream: "The organizing and educating of our children
for the defense of America, for the destruction of Hitlerism, will at the

same time aid in further democratizing the education of our children and the protection of their welfare. While we keep in mind the steps needed for full and basic improvement—we have to concentrate on the most immediate needs in the national defense efforts."[37]

The activities projected for the IWO Juniors were organizing paper drives, raising money for the USO, knitting socks for soldiers, and other efforts to build wartime morale. Thus the IWO, once committed to a revolutionary transformation of American life, like the Communist Party itself, was now committed to full participation in the national political culture in the interests of anti-Fascism.

When the United States entered the war following Pearl Harbor, the United States and the Soviet Union became allies. Many in the Communist world acted as if they believed that this wartime alliance could overcome radicals' alienation from America and secure a place for radicals within the dominant culture. Many Communists supported the dissolution of the Communist Party in 1944. They saw the effort to transform it into a nonrevolutionary "political association" as a way to claim a place in the political landscape of the United States after so many years of being marginalized and on the fringes. This turned out to be an illusion when the wartime tolerance turned into the postwar "Red Scare."

Even before the postwar disillusionment, the pro-American trend had a particularly negative effect on the children's activities. As the Juniors were increasingly engaged in activities similar to those of more mainstream children's and youth organizations, the attraction of the Juniors to radical parents decreased, as did its use to the radical movement. The Juniors were dissolved by the IWO in 1944; interestingly, at the same time that the Communist Party itself was dissolved.[38] The more that the Communist Party believed it could be in the mainstream of American culture, the less important it was for the Communists to maintain an organization designed to encourage the development of a separate, oppositional culture for their children.

The Jewish Shules and IWO Educational Programs

Among the Jewish sections of the IWO, the after-school programs, or *shules*, and summer camps were the most important IWO children's programs. The Juniors were never as important in the JPFO as they were for other sections.[39] The shules were founded in 1926 as the Non-Partisan Jewish Workers Schools in the first division between Communists and Socialists in the Workmen's Circle, and thus predated the founding of the IWO by four years.

In 1938, for example, even though the adult membership of the Jewish section was always the largest in the IWO, there were only 843 Jewish members of the IWO Juniors, but there were more than 2,000 children each belonging to the Slovak, Russian, English, and Polish Junior branches.[40]

The organization of children's schools was always seen as an important aspect of children's work within the IWO. Among many of the fraternal societies affiliated to the IWO, the children's schools were central to their efforts to pass on the ethnic culture and language of the parents. In addition to the shules of the Jewish sections, the Russian and Slovak sections also had strong after-school programs. The Russian Mutual Aid Society, which affiliated to the IWO in 1935,[41] had an entire nationwide system of after-school programs and Sunday schools, including high schools.[42] Finnish Communists also maintained a network of children's schools during this period, but the Finnish organization was not affiliated to the IWO until 1941. In 1946, the Cervantes Fraternal Society, the Spanish-language section of the IWO, planned to start schools in New York's Hispanic neighborhoods.[43] The IWO intended that the schools and the Juniors maintain a close and complementary relationship:

> It must be understood that the Junior Lodge is not a substitute for, does not replace the language school. . . .
>
> Where language schools exist, the closest relations should exist between the Junior Lodge and the school. Classes should be considered as constituent units of the Junior Lodge and should elect their delegates to the Junior Lodge executive.[44]

When the Non-Partisan Jewish Workers Schools began, they were similar to their Workmen's Circle counterparts. The emphasis in the curriculum was on Yiddish-language education and the discussion of social and political issues from the perspective of New York's Jewish working-class movement. Unlike the Workmen's Circle shules, the Non-Partisan Jewish Worker's Schools explicitly supported Communist politics, especially the Communist perspective on the Soviet Union, and were more overtly hostile toward Zionism and traditional religious beliefs in the Jewish community.

Between 1926 and the 1940s, the influence and popularity of the shules expanded. By December 1938, there were fifty-three IWO Jewish children's schools in New York City alone, attended by more than four thousand students. These included a kindergarten in the Bronx and three high schools, one each in Manhattan, the Bronx, and Brooklyn.[45] There were at least seven shules in both Philadelphia[46] and Chicago,[47] with others in New Jersey (Trenton, Passaic, and Paterson), New York (Syracuse), Detroit, Washington, D.C., and Los Angeles.[48]

Prior to 1936, the shules reflected much of the ideology of the Young Pioneer movement. Along with the revolutionism of the Pioneers, the curriculum of the shules paid attention to ethnicity in a way that foreshadowed the perspective of the IWO during the 1930s and 1940s.

In 1934, the Jewish section of the International Workers Order published a textbook for the third year of the schools. The text, designed to teach the Yiddish language, was written entirely in Yiddish. Most of the stories in the book were followed by vocabulary and grammar drills.

In 1951, the book was translated into English by the U.S. government during the investigation of the IWO. The ideology expressed in the book is hostile to both non-Communist Jewish ethnic life in the United States and to U.S. culture in general. However, its function as Yiddish-language text was part of an effort to preserve ethnicity within the radical movement and to introduce children growing up in an insular ethnic milieu to the Communist perspective on American life. Although the book was written in Yiddish, there is little in it that speaks to an autonomous Jewish culture in the United States. There are, however, a number of stories on Jewish life in the Soviet Union, as well as antireligious arguments against the "synagogue Jews." Indeed, the entire first section of the book is devoted to an antireligious story that criticizes and makes fun of religious Jews. In "Serke in the Worker's School" the institutions of the Communist culture are explicitly counterposed to those of the mainstream culture:

> Until Serke came to the Worker's School she knew nothing and understood nothing. The Public School teacher does not tell the children why there are classes [social classes—*translator's note*] in the world. Why does the landlord throw [the tenant] out from the apartment? Why is dad

unemployed? In Public School they teach other things, in Public School books—everything is written otherwise:

America is a free country, and Lincoln is the liberator of the Negroes. Now why do they lynch the "Blacks" in the South, why do they burn the "Blacks"? Why, and why, perhaps thousands of "whys" were asked by Serke, and the teacher was silent. Serke got sore at this whole business, until she understood—she is being taught lies.

So Serke came to the worker's school, met the children, got a book. Mother bought her a present: a red triangular scarf.[49]

Along with this story was the assignment to write a composition on the differences between the public school and the Worker's School, and to memorize a poem on the same subject whose last two lines were, "The school is a friend of the bosses and the millionaires. The school is an enemy of the workers and the pioneers."[50] This opposition between the school and the shule continues throughout the text.

The book also used the experiences of African Americans to illustrate the failures of American life, reflecting the increasing emphasis on this theme in the outlook of the Communist Party. Five out of the fourteen stories that focused on non-Jewish areas of American life dealt with the Black experience. The topics covered included the Scottsboro case, the trial of Angelo Herndon, and lynchings in the South. The other nine stories about American life mostly feature labor or radical martyrs such as the Haymarket martyrs, Ella Mae Wiggins (shot during the Gastonia strike), and Sacco and Vanzetti.[51]

Jewish themes in the text focused on the conflict between radical versus religious Jews or the comparison between Jewish life in the United States and Jewish life in the Soviet Union. The cultural, as well as political, alienation of Jewish Communists from American culture is apparent in many of the stories. In the segment "No More Movies" by Bertha Leltchuk, Hymie, the child of Communists begins to go to movies while his parents are out at meetings. The violence of the American movies gives him nightmares. He awakens at night crying after dreaming of being chased and shot at by men on horseback. The doctor says he has been made nervous by the movies. One day Hymie's parents take him to a movie, which surprises him. But it was a very different kind of movie: "There were no wild rides, and no shooting. He saw workers going to a desert, where there was nothing at all. There, they built factories, houses, and railroads. Then, workers were shown marching with banners and music."[52] This was a Soviet movie, and would presumably not give Hymie nightmares. The piece contains two moral lessons: The overt message points to the great differences between Soviet and American culture the author setting up a dichotomy between American, bourgeois fantasy adventure and Soviet documentary realism. The covert message speaks to parents' worries about providing a proper working-class education for their children, instructing them how to handle the fear that by going to meetings they were abandoning their children to the influences of bourgeois culture.

Over the course of the 1930s and 1940s, the IWO shules changed their curriculum as the Communist Party attempted to Americanize itself politically and to respond to the concerns of its political base. Rather than viewing ethnic allegiances as an unfortunate expression of political backwardness, Popular Front Communists began to celebrate ethnicity. To complement the CP slogan "Communism is Twentieth-Century Americanism," the IWO used the slogan "Americans All! Immigrants All!" Ernest Rymer, who at different times led both the Young Pioneers and the IWO Juniors, told me that the schools and children's organizations were a main source for this change: the people involved with the children's programs were the ones in the best position to hear parents' concerns.[53]

The switch did not occur without debate both within the IWO and the party. The debates within the Jewish sections of the IWO during the 1930s were often reminiscent of the debates in the Workmen's Circle during the 1910s and early 1920s. In the Workmen's Circle schools, the struggle had been between an assimilationist Socialist group that felt that any emphasis on Jewish subjects was a concession to "reactionary nationalism" and a group that wished to emphasize Jewish material; in the IWO, there was a general acceptance of the need to teach Jewish subjects, particularly Yiddish and Jewish history: what was debated was the context in which these subjects should be taught. On one side of this debate were those Jewish Marxists for whom the "progressive secular" education of the shules was part of a strategy to win Jewish workers to radical internationalism and participation in the ethnically and culturally diverse working-class movement. On the other side were people for whom this same "progressive secular" education was a way for Jewish Communists and other radicals to influence the multiclass Jewish community. Those identifying with the first perspective were seen as "cosmopolitans" ("assimilationists," by their adversaries); those on the other side were seen as veering dangerously close to "bourgeois" nationalism.[54]

By the 1940s, the shules of the IWO had become more identified with Jewish concerns. After the Second World War, Itche Goldberg, the national school and cultural director of the IWO, approached the Jewish Bureau of Education about affiliation for the IWO Jewish children's schools. Writing to the bureau, he explained his view of the purposes of the schools: "[These schools have] brought many thousands of young Jewish men and women . . . closer to the life of their people, who have gained a sense of deep understanding and meaning of their Jewishness, of the great tragedy and the great heroism which is their history, of the great sense of justice, of the great vision and hope for a better life which is their culture."[55]

The Bureau of Jewish Education applauded the recent changes in the IWO schools but rejected their application for affiliation on the grounds that the change was of such recent vintage: "It is but a short while ago that the IWO was not only openly antireligious and anti-Palestine, to the point of active persecution of religion and Zionism, but they had no regard whatever for classical Judaism, beginning the teaching of Jewish history and life with the Russian Revolution."[56]

Jewish Communists had tried to articulate a Jewish cultural life based in political radicalism, opposed to nationalism and religion with equal force, and based in their identification with the Soviet Union and their alliance with other ethnic left-wing groups. Thus they defined Jewish culture in terms of the class experiences of the Jewish working class, particularly in the needle trades, and saw the use of the Yiddish language as representing not simply Jewish culture but Jewish working-class culture.

This development and the debate that accompanied it took place in the context of changing circumstances for Jews, both internationally and domestically. The Nazi seizure of power in Germany occurred as the New Deal was helping to create a new middle class of Jewish educators and professionals. These second- and third-generation Jews knew little Yiddish and no longer lived in the Jewish working-class communities in which Jewish radicalism emerged.

In 1936, Arab uprisings directed against Jewish settlements in Palestine were supported by the CP as part of a legitimate national-liberation struggle. In 1939, the Moscow-Berlin Pact led the party to shift its emphasis from anti-Fascism to one opposing the preparations for an "imperialist" war. Furthermore, by the end of the war the Nazi extermination of the European Jewish community increasingly defined the Jewish American sense of ethnic identity. These events upset the delicate balance between ethnicity and universalism, and between *Yiddishkayt* and Marxism, that had been constructed by Jewish Communists during the 1920s and early 1930s. In their response to the war and to the changing conditions in the United States, children of working-class Jewish Communists wanted to become both more American and more Jewish.

CONCLUSION

The anti-Semitism of the Nazis affected Jews most strongly, but all left-wing nationality organizations faced a common problem: how to bridge the gap between the immigrant radical generation, whose political identification grew out of their experiences in Europe and in building ethnic communities in the United States, and their American-born, English-speaking children who identified politically as Americans. The fate of both their ethnic culture and their radical politics was at stake in this debate.

Between 1934 and 1944, the IWO in their junior section and other educational activities had attempted to create a radical political culture for children. The Communist organizers of the IWO hoped that the culture and politics of immigrant radicals would be passed on to their American-born children by emphasizing ethnic culture and traditions in a radical political framework. The organizers of the Juniors understood that the dissolution of ethnic ties, far from encouraging radicalism, as had been expected during the 1920s, would lead immigrant workers and their families away from radicalism. Those workers who maintained an interest in preserving their ethnic culture would have nowhere to turn but to the conservative ethnic organizations.

As this process developed, the IWO's celebration of ethnic culture became an end in itself, which in turn led to a de-emphasis of its separate radical identity. The IWO's retreat from radicalism was also due to the fact that by the end of the 1940s the adults in the IWO were frequently the children of immigrants, rather than immigrants themselves. They no longer spoke the native languages or had direct experience of the cultures of their parents.[57] For them, the strengthening of ethnic consciousness led not toward radicalism, but away from it. Their focus on their ethnic identities was a way of avoiding being swallowed up by America, but it also offered a way out of the extreme alienation from American society that had been part of their adherence to radical politics.

socialism in one summer

Radical Summer Camps in the 1930s and 1940s

Summertime is a utopian season. Children are freed from the constraints of school, the weather is cooperative, and the world belongs to kids. In the industrialized world, this "free" time has been extended to adults, for whom summer vacations provide welcome respite from the year's labor.

During the 1930s and 1940s, in summer camps, bungalow communities, and resorts, radicals used this freedom to create temporary communities organized around their own culture and values. These communities, temporary as they might be, were an extension of the spirit that animated the intentional communal settlements that flourished around the reform and radical movements of the late nineteenth and early twentieth centuries. For postwar Marxists, they were a way of participating in the radical American communitarian tradition.

The radical movement of this period spawned dozens of these institutions that functioned as both vacation resorts and utopian experiments. When the State of New York Legislative Committee on Charitable and Philanthropic Organizations investigated Communist camps in 1956, they found twenty-seven in that state alone.[1]

The Communist-oriented Left was not alone in organizing children's camps. Left-wing organizations not affiliated to the CP, including those opposed to the Communists, also organized such institutions. In 1927, the year after Kinderland's organizers separated from the Workmen's Circle (WC) to become part of the Communist-led

Non-Partisan Jewish Workers Schools, the WC built Kinder Ring, across Sylvan Lake from Kinderland[2]; the Pioneer Youth of America, an independent children's organization oriented to the socialist Left, had a camp at Rifton, New York, and another in North Carolina[3]; and the Highlander Folk School sponsored Junior Union camps as part of their support of trade union organizing in the South.[4] In 1919, the Sholom Aleichem Folk Institute, which had organized radical Yiddish-oriented children's programs in New York, started Camp Boiberik. That program pioneered what later would be instituted at both Kinderland and Kinder Ring—a summer program for children dedicated to a secular, socialist-oriented Yiddishkayt.[5]

By the late 1930s the Communists had become less critical of other left-wing institutions, and in 1939 the *New Pioneer* ran an article about summer camps for workers' children they believed their readers should consider. Along with Camp Kinderland and Wo-Chi-Ca, which were affiliated with the IWO, there were photographs of the Pioneer Youth Camp at Rifton and the anarchist Modern Sunday School camp.[6]

The network of summer camps and resorts that appealed to a Communist-oriented audience included those owned and operated by left-wing organizations such as the Fur and Leather Workers Union, the IWO, and privately run institutions. The formats varied: some camps were only for children; some resorts catered to adults and families; and some adult resorts had special programs for children. At Camp Unity, which began as an adult resort in 1924, by the end of the 1930s only the children's program remained. It was the same with Camp Wingdale.[7] The Goldensbridge and Mohegan Colonies had both permanent and summer residents.

At Camp Nitgedaigit an adult summer resort, Communists from New York created a space in which the culture they were creating in the city could be lived out freely, without the obstacles of living in a capitalist society. The camp was organized by residents of the United Workers Cooperative Houses in New York City in 1922.[8] The Yiddish name Nitgedaigit means "not to worry," although a State Police investigator claimed that it meant "Camp of Free Love"[9]—a designation not undeserved, according to people who remember it. Nitgedaigit allowed anyone who paid the $10 fee to join the cooperative and share in all decision making, even if they did not live in the cooperatives in New York. After a while, those who did live in the Coops wanted to have

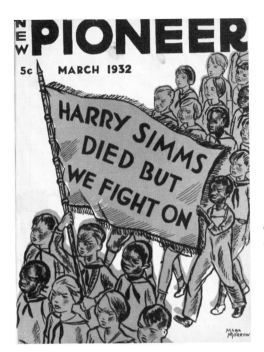

Cover of *New Pioneer* magazine (March 1932). (Harry Simms was a young YCL organizer killed while organizing for the National Miners Union.)

Cover of *Fairy Tales for Workers Children*.

Edith Segal rehearsing Ukrainian American Pioneer dance troupe. Courtesy of Shari Segal.

Children's marching band of the Mutualista Obrera (Puerto Rican section of the International Workers Order). From the Jesus Colon Papers. Courtesy of the Centro de Estudios Puertoriqueños, Hunter College–CUNY.

Graphic "Workers
Children Black and White
in the Pioneers Unite."
FROM *New Pioneer*
(OCTOBER 1932) BY LYDIA
GIBSON.

Find Lenin in *New Pioneer* (February 1933).

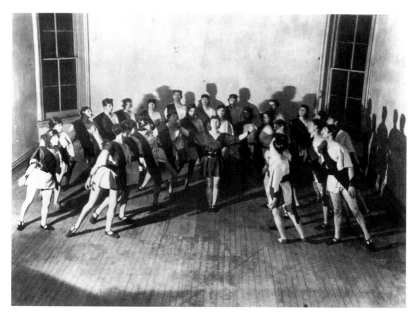

Edith Segal rehearsing children in dance program for Lenin Memorial Pageant ca. 1928. COURTESY OF SHARI SEGAL.

Kinderland Young Communist League branch in skit about the Spanish Civil War (1936). COURTESY OF MARVIN AND FLORENCE ITZKOWITZ. PHOTO BY BEN ITZKOWITZ.

Learning hour. Kinderland campers studying Yiddish (1936). COURTESY OF MARVIN AND FLORENCE ITZKOWITZ. PHOTO BY BEN ITZKOWITZ.

Pageant supporting an international antiwar congress. Skit about the French United Front (1935). COURTESY OF MARVIN AND FLORENCE ITZKOWITZ. PHOTO BY BEN ITZKOWITZ.

Kinderland campers demonstrate against 1936 Munich Olympics, 1935. COURTESY OF MARVIN AND FLORENCE ITZKOWITZ. PHOTO BY BEN ITZKOWITZ.

Madame Sholem Aleichem, widow of great Yiddish author visiting Kinderland (1937). COURTESY OF MARVIN AND FLORENCE ITZKOWITZ. PHOTO BY BEN ITZKOWITZ.

Pete Seeger singing with Woodland camper (nd). Courtesy of the Norman Studer Papers at the Hudson Valley Study Center, SUNY–New Paltz.

Woodland campers square dancing (nd). Courtesy of the Norman Studer Papers at the Hudson Valley Study Center, SUNY–New Paltz.

George Van Kleeck, traditional Hudson Valley singer with Woodland campers (nd). Courtesy of the Norman Studer Papers at the Hudson Valley Study Center, SUNY–New Paltz.

Paul Robeson and Edith Segal with young dancers. Courtesy of Shari Segel

more decision-making power, so in 1924 they left Nitgedaigit and founded Camp Unity. There was some competition between the two camps in the beginning.[10]

Life at Camp Nitgedaigit was the subject of a six-part series in the *New York World-Telegram* in August 1937. Although the series, "Comrades on Vacation," was meant as an exposé, it captures the feeling of the culture of a radical community.[11] In fact, the author, Elliott Arnold, seems to have some sympathy for his subjects. He wrote:

> Here, to a great degree, is Red Russia transplanted to America. Here are people who completely disavow all religion, and yet, during their stay here, practice, among themselves, an almost Christ-like "love-thy-neighbor" philosophy.
>
> These are some of the men and women who shove you in the subway, step on your toes in elevators, brush past you rudely on the streets. Yet here they achieve a sudden new behavior. They glorify Boy Scoutism and live in an almost Old Testament simplicity.[12]

Arnold was very attentive to the ways in which the beliefs, activities, and language of the campers created a bond among them. The bungalow doors were painted with hammers and sickles. There were meetings and the singing of revolutionary songs, and radical literature was sold. Vacationers were recruited for political work back in the city. In all these ways, Camp Nitgedaigit reflected the Communist hope for a revolutionary future.

Arnold noted how the word *comrade* had a special meaning at Nitgedaigit.

> To address another as "comrade" at Nitgedaigit was more than social convention. It was an expression of the common bond created by a shared political faith.
>
> Something should be said here about the fetishism made of the word "comrade." It is a word you hear spoken most frequently, and it means much more to them than the uninitiated can comprehend.
>
> It is not another way of saying "friend" or "mister" to them. It is rather an expression of spiritual kinship. It is the establishment of a psychic bond between the user and the one it is used on. The word is used to express meanings these men and women have made for themselves. One day this writer was walking up a steep hill with a man and a

woman. Both are party members. The woman was having difficulty walking up the incline. She called to the man:

"Comrade, give me a hand."

He turned and looked at her and smiled a close secret smile. Then he extended his hand and said:

"Here it is. Take it."

He helped her up. For a moment they held their hands together.[13]

The utopian and socially experimental character of the summer communities was more focused in the children's camps. The children's camp organizers hoped that with children, rather than adults, they could better resolve the contradiction between the present-day world of capitalism and the envisioned future of socialism. Thus the radical summer camps for children were ideal locations for putting into practice the visionary aspects of the Communist culture.

The Communist-oriented children's summer camps organized during the era of the Popular Front were more diverse in style and content than had been the camps of the Young Pioneers and the WIR during the 1920s. In those camps there was a unitary vision, often inspired by practices in the Soviet Union; the camps were, thus, organized around a purely political conception. By the 1930s, the camps began to address new questions regarding the relationship between the radical movement and American culture. This prompted greater diversity between camps and more experimentation in the camp programs.

The IWO and other groups allied with the Communist Party organized children's summer camps throughout the 1930s and 1940s, even into the 1950s. Some continued or grew out of camps begun during the 1920s. Others began as children's programs at left-wing adult resorts, and some were organized from scratch. As in the 1920s, they expressed the culture of the particular configuration of the Communist or radical movement in the areas in which they were built. For example, Camp Robin Hood, which was started near Cleveland in 1938, was founded by representatives of the Hungarian Singing Society, the Bakery Drivers Auxiliary of Locals 52 and 56, the Finnish Women's Society, the Progressive Women's Council, and the Finnish Educational Society, and was endorsed by the District Council of the United Auto Workers Union and the United Labor Congress.[14] By the Fifth National Convention of the IWO, four districts had children's camps: New York,

Philadelphia, Cleveland, and Chicago. Later, additional camps were organized in Massachusetts, California, Detroit, and Minneapolis.[15]

Camps organized by groups or individuals involved in the Communist Party orbit and that drew upon Communist circles reflected a multilayered approach to the creation of a radical political culture for children. Like the summer camps of the late 1920s, they attempted to provide a practical expression of a radical vision of the new community. The aim of the camps was, as a Kinderland director said, to build "the real patriots of the future."[16]

The three radical children's camps in New York State that I explore below particularly exemplify diversity: Kinderland, Camp Wo-Chi-Ca, and Camp Woodland. Looking at them from the early 1930s to the early 1950s illustrates different ways in which the tensions between Communist politics and the immigrant and American cultures was confronted.

All three camps bear the earmarks of the peculiarities of the New York City–based radical movement of the time, in particular the Jewish working-class and lower-middle-class constituency of the Communist movement. Although these camps had much in common with each other, their differences illustrate three different routes that American radicals could take in forming a political culture for children that would reflect their social and political values. During this period, as mentioned earlier, camps set up elsewhere expressed particular regional characteristics. The New York camps, however, because they were so numerous, show more clearly the diversity that was possible—that was in fact encouraged—within the Communist movement. At that time, camps elsewhere may have displayed aspects, and combinations of aspects, that it was possible, in New York, to develop more discretely.

Because of the strength of the Communist Party among Jews in New York City, all left-wing institutions in the New York region bore the stamp of ethnic Jewish culture. In the children's summer camps this was expressed in a variety of ways. Indeed, the very notion of ethnic pluralism as it became developed in the Communist movement owes much to a long-term Jewish project of maintaining the Jewish culture and traditions within a non-Jewish world. In the Communist Left, this Jewish perspective was expanded to encompass all ethnic groups. Furthermore, the radical effort to be "in the world but not of it" may, as Daniel Bell points out, reflect the long-term influence of the Jewish

Marxist-oriented Left more than that of Marxism per se.[17] Of the three camps I explore here, Kinderland emphasized the maintenance and development of a Jewish ethnic culture most explicitly, but all of them emphasized ethnic pluralism as a social goal.

Kinderland began in 1923 and is still in existence. It was a center for the development of a secular Jewish radicalism. The camp program was committed to the transmission to children of Eastern European Jewish immigrants of a radical *Yiddishkayt,* the secular Jewish culture created by radical, working-class Jewish workers in the needle trades. Wo-Chi-Ca (a name formed from the abbreviation of Workers Children's Camp) became noted for its attention to the English-speaking children of radical immigrants and their efforts to build a camp around Black-white solidarity. Woodland, although not directly sponsored by radical organizations as were Kinderland and Wo-Chi-Ca, pioneered the effort to make American folk culture, particularly folk music, the basis for a radical political culture.

The adults who organized and staffed these camps hoped that they would be vehicles for transmitting their values to their children, and in each case they created a small experiment where this could occur. The camps were arenas where culture was created, not simply educational institutions, because of the relationship between the organized educational activities and the space between the organized activities. In this space, children created their own "feeling" for the camps. The informal and undirected times were as politically important as activities directed toward communicating a specific political message. To feel comfortable, in their own setting, was a unique experience for the children of radicals, whose families' values were at odds with those of the dominant culture. The programs and activities of the camp promoted values and an ideology in tune with the beliefs the children were taught at home. At the same time, the absence of hostility toward those beliefs became one of the utopian elements in the camps.

Kinderland, Wo-Chi-Ca, and Woodland all attempted to contribute to the development of a critical perspective in children vis-à-vis American life. The camps' common origins in the Communist-oriented radical movement led to certain similarities in their outlook and programs. For example, the themes of combating ethnic and racial bigotry, promoting interethnic and interracial cooperation, and teaching children to support the labor movement were common to all three camps.

Nevertheless, each camp should be seen as a separate project, reflecting diverse values and concerns. Organized by different segments in the Communist milieu, the camps reflect very different conceptions of the nature of a radical political culture. Each camp attempted to create an experience for children that would, in itself, reflect the values the organizers saw as central.

Camp Kinderland

Camp Kinderland, founded in 1923 by activists in the *shules* of the Workmen's Circle, was located on Sylvan Lake in Dutchess County, New York. An adult resort, Lakeland, was attached to the children's camp during much of Kinderland's history. The relationship between the camp and the shules in the city was always central to the organizers' conception of Kinderland. The principle "*Foon shule in kemp, foon kemp in shule*" (from shule to camp, from camp to shule) expressed the continuity between the Yiddish cultural activities in the city and the activities in camp.[18]

Historians of the Workmen's Circle claim that the Communists "stole" Kinderland from the Workmen's Circle after the left-right split in the organization in 1926.[19] The founders of the camp claim, however, that the Workmen's Circle was never actually involved in the camp at all. Yankl Doroshkin, one of the three founders of the camp, wrote in 1979 that the camp was organized by activists in the Workmen's Circle, but that the organization itself refused any financial support or sponsorship.[20]

When the Workmen's Circle shules split along Communist-Socialist lines in 1926, three years before the organization itself divided along similar lines, Kinderland was firmly in the hands of left-wing and Communist elements. The next year, when the Workmen's Circle opened Camp Kinder Ring across Sylvan Lake, the two camps engaged in much verbal rivalry, but also some cooperation, over the course of their histories.[21]

Kinderland was an independent institution operating within the milieu of the Communist-allied Jewish working-class movement in New York. After the formation of the IWO, it was formally sponsored by the Jewish People's Fraternal Order of the IWO. The organizers, management, and staff of the camp were drawn from the radical movement in New York, although once at Kinderland, for many of them, the camp became their primary political/cultural area of activity. Yankl Doroshkin wrote, "During the 14 years that I was associated with Kinderland, the camp was for us a holy mission."[22]

Daily life for campers at Kinderland was organized around activities that were a combination of structured and unstructured time. In the morning, after breakfast and the clean-up of the bunks, there was often an early assembly. In the first years of the camps this was a salute to the Red Flag, but during the 1930s this was changed to a less ritualized, more informal ceremony in which the campers gathered, grouped according to age, each group carrying colored banners that often bore Yiddish slogans. The days were divided into a typical summer camp program of swimming, sports, and play, plus educational and cultural activities directed toward the camp's political goals. Yiddish classes were mandatory through the 1930s and much of the cultural life was organized around the teaching of Yiddish culture and the history of Eastern European and U.S. working-class Jews.

What might seem to be normal activity for a child's summer camp was politicized by its context in the educational and cultural programs. These were integral to the camp. Classes and formal discussions were conscientiously carried out by the camp organizers. But equally important were the celebrations and rituals marking special events and holidays.

When prominent figures from the radical movement visited the camp, everything was organized to mark the importance of the occasion. The bunk rooms were cleaned especially well. Dramatic presentations, dances, and songs were rehearsed for presentation to the visitors. When the VIP arrived, the entire camp turned out in what was called a "white salute": all the children dressed in white except for colored neckerchiefs signifying their age group. Campers carried banners with Yiddish slogans, the symbol of Kinderland, or portraits of notable Yiddish cultural figures such as Sholom Aleichem, I. L. Peretz, or Morris Rosenberg.

Accounts of the visits of Madam Sholom Aleichem (the widow of the writer), Itzak Feffer (the Soviet Yiddish writer), and Paul Robeson show the importance of these occasions in the life of Kinderland. These three people further demonstrate the contours of the secular Jewish radical culture that Kinderland was attempting to create.

When Madam Sholom Aleichem visited Kinderland, in summer 1937, the event was a very significant event for the camp. Sholom Aleichem was revered throughout the Jewish community in the United States for his stories about Jewish life in the mythical Eastern European village of Kasrilevke. His writings expressed the ways in which life in the shtetls of Eastern Europe had influenced the culture of immigrant Jews in the United States. Like most writers and intellectuals of the Yiddish world, Aleichem had been a socialist sympathizer. However, he died before the divisions that split the Jewish radical movement had become hardened. The visit of his widow to Kinderland signified that the camp had a legitimate place in the Jewish community as a whole. It also represented the claim that their particular brand of Jewish radicalism was the heir to the Yiddishist radical traditions of the period preceding the First World War. It was as if they had received Sholom Aleichem's posthumous blessing.

Camper Edith Sadowsky's description gives some of the flavor of Madame Sholom Aleichem's visit:

> The other day all was a hustle and bustle in Camp Kinderland preparing to have everything ready to greet Madam Sholom Aleichem, the wife of the great Jewish humorist, Sholom Aleichem. All the children in camp first saw Madam Sholom Aleichem when she entered the dining room. She is a woman of the age of seventy-five, with white hair and wrinkled face but she gave us a sweet and comradely impression. As she entered the dining room, she was given a yell by the spirited campers who were glad to see her.
>
> The next morning we had a salute to her husband. The different bungalows impersonated different characters in his stories. Speeches were made by the directors and Madam Sholom Aleichem made a speech also. Then the monument erected to her husband was unveiled and she was so touched that she cried.[23]

The visits of Itzak Feffer and Paul Robeson were accompanied by similar presentations and meetings. Feffer, one of the best-known Soviet Yiddish writers, was executed by Stalin in the late 1940s; however, in the 1930s the prominence achieved by Feffer and fellow-writer Isaac Babel represented the Soviet solution to the problems of anti-Semitism; it was the creation of a secular Jewish culture in a socialist context.[24]

Singer/activist Paul Robeson had equal importance in that he represented the American culture, of which the Jewish radicals were attempting to become a part. Sholom Aleichem and Itzak Feffer were representatives of worlds very distant from that in which Kinderlanders lived—
one was distant in time, the other in space—and it was because their
relationship with American life was most important and most difficult
that Robeson's visits were of particular importance. He was greeted in a
fashion similar to that accorded to the others.

Among the most important ritual occasions at Kinderland were the
campers' dramatic and dance presentations on political or historical
themes. Both the presentation and its preparation were important
parts of the Kinderland experience and they occupy a major place in
many of the memories that children took with them from camp. The
figure responsible for these events was the dancer Edith Segal,[25] the
dance teacher at Kinderland and at the shules of the IWO throughout
the 1930s. The daughter of Jewish immigrants, she grew up on New
York's Lower East Side and was introduced to modern dance at the
Henry Street Settlement House. During the 1920s she studied with
Martha Graham. At the same time that she was being introduced to
modern dance, she began to attend classes on socialism at the Rand
School. In addition to teaching in the children's camps and the shules,
she directed the Red Dancers Group and the Nature Friends Dance
Group. Her life was spent weaving together modern dance and politi-
cal radicalism.

In 1924, while hitchhiking across the country, Segal was in Chicago
when news came of Lenin's death. At the memorial organized by the
Communist Party, she danced the *Worker's Funeral March* and the
Internationale (her accompanist was Rudolf Liebisch, a Chicago musician who had played the funeral march at Joe Hill's funeral nine years
earlier). Returning to New York, Segal organized a dance group with
members of the Young Pioneers (six girls and one boy). Some of her earliest choreography for children was for a Pioneer dance group she
directed in an expanded version of her Chicago dances at the Lenin
Pageant in New York in 1928.[26]

At Kinderland, Segal's choreography combined the expressive loose-
ness of modern dance with the more structured folk dances of Eastern
Europe, united around a political concept. This had roots in the work
of the Workers' Dance League, founded in 1932, that joined the dance

groups of the Needle Trades Industrial Union and the Furriers Union with the Red Dancers and the Harlem Dance Group. Their first recital used folkdance as well as modern dance forms.[27] At Kinderland, Segal taught dance and choreographed presentations and pageants.

An example of her work was the program "Immigrants All! Americans All!" performed at Kinderland in the summer of 1939. Lawrence Emery covered it for the *Daily Worker*:

> It was done in costume, and to the rhythm of beating drums and blasting bugles in the children's own band. Beginning with a group of beleathered Indians, the kids staged a lively procession of events and peoples and they drove home the point that America is what people from other lands have made it—the French and the Spanish, the English and the Dutch, the Irish and the Russian, the Negro and the Hungarian, the Jew and the Gentile, Lafayette, Kosciusko, and Haim Solomon were all there and it was clear that no race or nationality can be excluded from the democracy that they built as Americans.[28]

Emery noted that there were plans for pageants on the Jews in American history that would trace Jewish involvement in radical causes from antislavery to the union organizing drives of the twentieth century. Ending his article, Emery wrote that "a lot of little Jewish-American boys and girls are getting their first glimpse of the world of tomorrow, and it is a world that draws on the best of the past for its creation."[29]

Segal was able to use modern dance to confront some of the tensions that existed for children growing up in the radical Jewish culture in which she, too, lived. Children of radical immigrant parents needed a way not only to be involved in their parents' world but, somehow, to make it their own. Her dances contained two very important parts of this process. Because dance does not depend on verbal presentation, Segal's choreography offered an occasion for both children and adults to participate in a symbolic expression of their common beliefs. These dances were not expressions of radical ideology per se, but were the radical outlook distilled into action and gesture. This outlook could be shared between the generations precisely because it was the spirit of radicalism that was being expressed, rather than particulars of political strategy. Further, in modern dance, children at Kinderland were exposed to the forms of self-expression that were increasingly important aspects of American child rearing. Segal's enthusiasm was infectious, and she was able to carry along with her both children and adults.

The cultural life at Kinderland and Lakeland were a focus for an entire cultural movement operating within the Jewish Communist milieu of New York City. Actors from Artef, the Yiddish theater group, and singers from Yiddish choral groups, the Freiheit Gesang Verein, were staff members at the camps. They, too, helped create the cultural presentations that were such an important part of camp life. In the 1940s, cultural figures who were moving from the cultural world of the Left into the mainstream were involved with Lakeland and Kinderland. These included film director Jules Dassin, composer Robert DeCormier, actor Zero Mostel, and musician Mercer Ellington.

The Jewish Communist culture that was nurtured and expanded at Kinderland was historically grounded in the experiences of the Jewish working class of prerevolutionary Russia and of the New York City of the 1900s to the 1930s. The cultural materials of the past were used to project their vision of the future—a future personified by their children. The vision was of an American socialism grounded in the Yiddish language and the cultural life of the Jewish working class.

CAMP WO-CHI-CA

Wo-Chi-Ca, founded in 1936, grew in the same soil as Kinderland, but its focus was less on the culture created by immigrants and more on a Popular Front–era Communist conception of American democracy. Although many of the children who attended Wo-Chi-Ca came from New York Jewish families similar to those of children at Kinderland, the organizers of Wo-Chi-Ca did not attempt to keep the Yiddish language of the parents alive at the camp. Instead, they attempted to translate the experiences of the Communist culture in New York—predominantly Jewish though it was—into an American socialist vision that would reflect the concerns of a multiethnic and multiracial working class. Interracialism was, thus, a central theme at Wo-Chi-Ca. Camp organizers hoped that by creating an institution where Black and white children would interact on a daily basis, racism could be confronted openly and overcome.

Wo-Chi-Ca was founded by people who had been active in the Young

Pioneers, the IWO Juniors, and other sections of the radical children's movement in New York. The idea came from people who had been involved in Camp Wingdale, New York, a Communist adult camp.[30] The founding group included both members of the Communist Party and nonmembers. According to Ernest Rymer, the camp's first director, the people who founded Wo-Chi-Ca—located on 150 acres of land in Port Murray, New Jersey—wanted to provide a camping experience for their children that would not be as ethnically specific as Kinderland.[31]

Some of the differences between Wo-Chi-Ca and Kinderland were as much a result of physical necessity as ideology. There were no buildings and no facilities on the land when the camp opened. The first summer, campers lived in tents and participated in the construction of the first camp buildings—dining areas, bunks, and the waterfront. What began as a necessity soon turned into a virtue, for it was thought that there could be no better way to teach children the dignity of labor and the importance of cooperative, unexploited labor than to make work one of the basic activities of the camp. This aspect of Wo-Chi-Ca continued into the 1940s, although gradually the work camp became only a special group within the larger camp.[32]

In the 1930s and 1940s, the idea of interracial camping for children was daring. Most children's camps were de facto segregated because of their sponsorship by all-white organizations such as churches and fraternal organizations, and in addition, the cost of sending a child to camp was prohibitive for most Black families. There was also constant opposition to interracial camping from conservatives in the state. When the radical summer camps were under investigation in the 1950s, the integrated nature of the camps was seen as important by both anti-Communists and those involved in the camps. The camps were often harassed by people who shouted not only anti-Communist and anti-Semitic slogans, but racist slurs as well. During the New York State investigation of Communist-influenced summer camps, Elton and Sarah Gustafson, who ran a private camp, Timberline, issued a statement to the committee in which they warned that "every person called for investigation before this committee represents an interracial camp; it is difficult to conceive of this as accidental."[33] Indeed, of all the integrated camps in New York State, only a few settlement-house camps and the Pioneer youth camp were not investigated.

Wo-Chi-Ca's program was a manifestation of how children of

immigrants attempted to construct an American version of the immigrant radical culture of earlier periods. Antiracism and an emphasis on the role of African Americans in U.S. society were central components of this project. At Wo-Chi-Ca, both Black and white children could live and play together in an approximation of a community in which the walls between the two races had been broken down.

In 1944, IWO Lodge 500 held an evening of music and dance to help the camp. Two Blacks, singer Hazel Scott and dancer Pearl Primus, the dance teacher at Wo-Chi-Ca, put on a benefit performance. The preshow publicity announcement begins: "Negro and white youngsters who will take possession of the new bungalows at worker's children's Camp Wo-Chi-Ca in New Jersey. . . . "[34] It quoted Pearl Primus:

"As children, we carry deep in our hearts the richest of human affections, free from bigotry and hate. We must help our children grow up with this affection strengthened. We owe it to them. And that is why we must be generous when it comes to helping organizations that help children. That is why I will dance for Camp Wo-Chi-Ca and that is why you should come to see me dance."[35]

The white families who sent their children to Wo-Chi-Ca were predominantly Jewish. However, by the 1940s children from other ethnic backgrounds also began to attend Wo-Chi-Ca in significant numbers. The camper list from 1949 includes many Latin American, Slovak, and Italian names, in addition to Jewish ones.[36] In 1938, Congressman Vito Marcantonio sponsored four Puerto Rican children from his East Harlem district, including future Salsa musician Tito Puente.[37]

As radicalism emerged from its concentration in ethnic communities, interracialism defined radical culture for those families that sent their children to Wo-Chi-Ca. African Americans, like Jews, were outsiders in their own land. They were also native-stock Americans. For radicals of immigrant backgrounds, the Black experience in the United States allowed them to identify with an aspect of American life and culture without being absorbed into an unsympathetic mainstream. Apparently, the inverse was true for Blacks who found their way to the radical movement during this period, particularly to the Communist movement: among the Jewish radicals from immigrant backgrounds, Blacks could find white people who carried little or none of the racist baggage of American-born whites, particularly Southerners. Jews were white people with whom Blacks could have interracial experiences without a history of extreme racism hanging over them. This is not to say that Black-white relationships in these institutions were devoid of tensions; even the organizers of Wo-Chi-Ca admitted there were problems. They claimed, however, that at Wo-Chi-Ca "relationships and problems are not glossed over, but are met and discussed. Out of this process grows close understanding and unbiased companionship."[38] Furthermore the staff at Wo-Chi-Ca was always interracial. Dancer Pearl Primus was not the only prominent African American artist who worked at the camp. Jacob Lawrence, the painter, ran the art program, and he and his wife painted murals at the camp dining hall.[39]

One way in which interracialism was practiced at Wo-Chi-Ca was to make African American culture representative of American culture in general. Songs from the Black tradition were sung and skits illustrating the experiences of Black people in the United States were performed. These were important parts of the camp program, along with songs and skits drawn specifically from the European radical tradition, such as the songs of the Spanish Civil War and skits based on the history of the U.S. labor movement.

At Wo-Chi-Ca, as at Kinderland, Paul Robeson was an important symbol of the effort to unite these two streams of American protest; the labor movement and the African American's struggle. Not only were Robeson's dignity and personal accomplishments enormous, he had pro-Soviet and anticolonialist sympathies. In addition, Paul Robeson Jr. attended Wo-Chi-Ca during the summers of 1941 and 1942.[40]

The *Wo-Chi-Ca Yearbook* of 1949 devoted three pages to "Paul Robeson Day" when Robeson visited the camp on 17 August 1949:

> When Paul Robeson came there was great excitement. Everyone was pushing and screaming. I had never seen Paul before. He was tall and friendly looking, and had a broad smile, . . .
>
> We met him in front of the infirmary. He went in front of the Main House, and there was everybody trying to see him through the windows and doors.[41]

At an all-camp assembly after lunch, campers performed skits and Robeson made a speech and sang. By far, the most important activity took place after the assembly. Unlike Kinderland, where visitors were greeted with formal ceremonies and presentations, Wo-Chi-Ca adopted a most

American way: Robeson umpired a baseball game between two teams of camp staff members. Noticeable in the description of the game is the informality of the occasion. Camper Serge Kanevsky wrote: "The game was a hilarious comedy from beginning to end. Paul Robeson did a fine job of calling balls and strikes. One of the unusual features of this umpiring was the fact that Paul was able to call the pitch before the ball left the pitcher's hand. . . . The game was played in an atmosphere of friendship which helped make the game enjoyable for each staff member as well as for the spectators."[42]

Other visitors to Wo-Chi-Ca included the artist Rockwell Kent, who served as the president of the IWO, and Ella Reeve "Mother" Bloor, one of the best-known Communist women.

Wo-Chi-Ca also emphasized support for and identification with the labor movement. The 1949 yearbook listed the unions to which the parents of campers belonged,; they included unions representing clothing workers, carpenters, electrical workers, furriers, department store workers, teachers, office workers, and transport workers, and others.[43] In the *Wo-Ki-Mag*, a magazine produced by campers during the off-season, a Labor Day editorial emphasized the importance of the labor movement for Wo-Chi-Ca and described how support for the labor movement had been developed at the camp the previous summer:

> We have instituted the Wo-Chi-Ca Council for Industrial Organization. We have attempted through this medium to bring home to ourselves some of the meaning of trade unionism, some conception of the goals for which our fathers have fought, been jailed, and shed blood. Every camper at Wo-Chi-Ca has been a union member, every activity shack in Wo-Chi-Ca has been a union shop, and every counselor has tried to instill in the minds of his charges the dignity of labor and respect for the work of others.[44]

In 1945, campers at Wo-Chi-Ca were asked to express their ideas on the meaning of Wo-Chi-Ca and what they hoped for the future. These were collected and published in the camp's reunion book under three categories: Personal Freedoms, a Bill of Racial Equality, and the World of Tomorrow. Among the personal freedoms campers thought important were "the right of boys and girls to work, play and grow up together," "the right of people to live and work together regardless of race, religion or creed," and "the right to change things, the right to

love, the right to retain one's own identity."[45] Entered in the Bill of
Racial Equality were:

> We believe that all children of all different origins, here in America—
> Jewish and Gentile, Negro and white, European and Asiatic—should live
> together, play together, sleep under the same roofs, share things together.
>
> We believe that the Ghettos and Chinatowns and Harlems should
> disappear and that all people should live in good houses and that the peo-
> ple of different colored skins should live in the same house. . . .
>
> In order to help carry out these beliefs we pledge ourselves to keep
> racial equality in our camp and to try to spread the idea of racial equal-
> ity wherever we go.
>
> We pledge ourselves to combat the influence of jokes, comic books,
> newspapers, radio programs that make fun of any people.[46]

For the World of Tomorrow, the campers envisioned a city where the
ideals of racial equality, the end of poverty and unemployment, and victory over fascism were all brought together. Workers and farmers,
Black and white, people from all over the world would live in security
and cooperation: "This is our future. This is the future for which we
fight. This is the future we will attain!"[47]

Wo-Chi-Ca was forced to close in the mid-1950s, harassed by its
neighbors. It merged with Camp Wyandot, a left-oriented, interracial
camp whose directors had ties with Wo-Chi-Ca through an organization
called the Inter-Racial Camp Fund.[48]

CAMP WOODLAND

Camp Woodland, in Phoenicia, New York, in the Catskill Mountains,
drew on some of the experiences of other radical camps but forged a
third alternative for the creation of a radical culture: it linked an urban-
based radicalism with the "naturally" democratic traditions of rural
America.

Camp Woodland, founded in 1938 and closed in 1962, was run by
people whose ties to the radical movement were not primarily with the
associations and organizations of the Communist Left. Rather, they had
worked within the left-wing of the Progressive Education movement.
It was therefore not organizationally affiliated to the radical movement,

as were Kinderland and Wo-Chi-Ca, but drew its staff and campers from the radical world.

During the 1930s, a number of teachers involved in the Progressive Education movement became attracted to the political Left, in particular to the Communist Party. It seemed to them that their goal of social reconstruction through education would be impossible to achieve without radical political reconstruction as well.

The relationship between political radicalism and Progressive Education goes back to before the First World War. Yet in the early 1930s, Communists were critical of Progressive Education, as such. They were far more concerned with the ideological content of the curriculum in public schools and the question of access to good schools for working-class children than they were with small-scale experiments in educational methods. In a pamphlet on the state of the schools during the Great Depression in 1934, Communist writer Rex David wrote: "The Progressive Education Association stands for all that is new and 'progressive' in teaching. Their 'liberal' leaders have made genuine advances in developing methods and materials to protect and develop the children in their care. But their support comes from private schools and wealthy communities. They are as weak and supine in the struggle against attacks on the public schools as the N.E.A. and the state associations."[49]

The critique of Progressive Education by Communist writers on education did not halt the movement of educators toward a Marxist analysis and political sympathy with the Communist Party. As the Communist Party moved into the Popular Front phase in which it sought alliances with liberals, and as it began recruiting members from among teachers and educational professionals, it became more open to the efforts of Progressive Education. This development of a mutual sympathy took place at two levels. On the one hand, the work of George Counts and the group around his journal *Social Frontiers* was an attempt to extend the analysis that had been part of the Progressive Education tradition into new, more political directions. Out of this trajectory came two books that presented a Marxist analysis of education: Howard Langford's *Education and the Social Conflict* (1936)[50] and Zalmen Slesinger's *Education and the Class Struggle* (1937).[51] Both authors came out of the Progressive Education tradition. Slesinger was more critical of the efforts of Progressive educators than was Langford, but both shared an interest in the idea that schools could become instru-ments of radical social change.[52]

While this was occurring in the area of educational theory, a similar process was taking place within the progressive schools, particularly in New York City and the surrounding area. Communists and their allies began to participate in these schools as parents, teachers, and adminis-trators. Communists were active at Hessian Hills School at Croton-on-Hudson and at New York City's Walden School, the Little Red School House, Elizabeth Irwin High School, and the Downtown Community School.

Norman Studer, the founder and director of Camp Woodland throughout its history, had been a Ph.D. student of John Dewey's at Columbia University when the Depression cut short his academic career. In 1932, he became a teacher at the Little Red School House. In 1951, he became the director of the Downtown Community School and main-tained that position until the school closed in 1970.[53] When Woodland was investigated in 1955, Studer took the Fifth Amendment when he was asked about his membership in the Communist Party. However, it is clear that he had many ties with the Communist world.[54] In 1926, he had written an article for the *New Masses* on "The Revolt in the American Colleges," and while teaching at the Little Red School House during the 1930s he had taken his students to Communist May Day parades.[55]

The Downtown Community School under Studer is an example of the participation of Communists in a Progressive Education setting. It was founded in 1944 by parents interested in providing quality, interra-cial education for their children. Among the people identified with the Communist movement who had children in the school in the late 1940s and early 1950s were lawyer Leonard Boudin, Charles Hendley, president of the New York Teachers Union, Tass news agency writer Franklin Folsom, the Black folksinger Josh White, Simon Gerson, edi-tor of the *Daily Worker*, and V. J. Jerome, editor of the Communist Party's theoretical journal *Political Affairs*. Pete Seeger was a music teacher; Rockwell Kent was a sponsor; and Lillian Hellman was on the board of trustees.[56]

Many liberals, too, were involved in the school, including Margaret Mead (Mead actually withdrew from her involvement in the school and took her daughter Cathy out of it when charges of Communist influence became strong in the early 1950s). Other liberals were the Reverend

Edward Carroll and Mrs. Louise Gimbel of the department store family. The school was a parent-teacher cooperative, which gave radicals a strong voice there.[57]

Norman Studer described how Camp Woodland emerged from both the Progressive Education tradition and the socially critical climate of the 1930s:

> The camp was part of a widespread movement of reform that was not new in American life, but which grew to special importance in the late 1930s and 1940s.
>
> . . . The democratic ethos, the ideals of the founding fathers, half expressed in the Constitution, but never brought to fruition for Blacks, Women and Trade Unionists were being proclaimed for all by poets, philosophers and scientists. The people who founded Camp Woodland believed in this new education. They went further than most educators and linked the liberation of children firmly with the new emerging culture of democracy. For us, the new "progressive Education" meant more than new methods in the classroom. It meant the creation of a new personality to fit the new kind of culture which we saw developing in America.[58]

At the time that Woodland was founded in 1939, the patterns of work, leisure, and family life in the rural communities of New York State had many continuities with life during the nineteenth century and before. Further—and this was central to the goals of Camp Woodland—these communities could be seen as residual expressions of an almost-lost American democratic spirit.[59] Camp Woodland's organizers thought that if children were taken from the city and placed in the rural Catskill setting, they would learn about the lives and activities of the local inhabitants, at the same time sharing with the residents the experience of living in the city. The camp was interracial from the beginning and made great efforts to maintain both Black and white children as campers.

This relationship between the camp and its neighbors, in which the directors and staff at Woodland projected a vision of an American radicalism grounded in American democratic traditions, was not simple romanticism. It was not just an American version of "going to the people." The idea was to construct a historically grounded vision of the possibilities of life in the United States drawing upon urban radicalism and rural traditionalism. Woodlanders were expected to teach something to the country people as well as learn from them—through the structure of camp democracy, the interracial/intercultural emphasis of the camp, and the engagement of the camp's neighbors in the revival and continuation of their own cultural traditions. The realization of the Woodland vision was dependent on this dialogic process. In a statement summing up the goals of the camp, a Woodland promotional brochure proclaimed:

> Camp Woodland is coeducational and interracial. Children learn the democratic way of life by actually living it. The genuine quality of camp democracy is attested to by the comment of an old Catskill lumberman, who exclaimed after seeing the camp in operation:
>   "If someone had told me that there was a place where all peoples lived and worked together I wouldn't have believed it—it's just wonderful."[60]

From the start, the organizers of Woodland attempted to build relationships with their Catskills neighbors on a basis of respect and understanding. By showing an appreciation for the lifeways of the people around them, it was hoped that rural people would, in turn, develop a respect for the ways of the city folk who had come among them. The yearbook of the camp was entitled *Neighbors: A Record of Catskill Life,* and each issue contained examples of the relationships developed in Woodland between the city children and the camp's rural neighbors.[61]

The centerpiece of this program was the effort to bring people from the rural communities around the camp to share stories, songs, and life histories with the children. Examples of this abound. George Edwards, an old woodsman from Roscoe, New York, was a frequent visitor at the camp. He taught many songs with long histories in the Catskills, which were later recorded by the Library of Congress Folk Music Collection.[62] A raftsman, Orson Slack, who was eighty-two years of age in 1948, told stories about lumbering and rafting on the Hudson, and the village blacksmith of Sampsonville, George Van Kleeck, called the weekly square dances at the camp.

Out of these activities, a museum of Catskill Work Tools was assembled at the camp to preserve traditional work implements of country life. An annual summer folk festival was begun at which singers and storytellers from nearby towns were joined by urban folk interpreters—among them Pete Seeger—and folklorists and collectors such as Norman Cazden and Herbert Haufrecht.

The city children were also put into contact with the experiences of country life through the many excursions they made in the surrounding countryside. During these trips they explored local history and the culture of the region. During the late 1940s, camp plays were produced based on these explorations. *Action on Dingle Hill* told of the eighteenth-century anti-rent wars that took place in the area around Woodland. More contemporary problems addressed included the building of the Lackawack Dam, which drowned a number of villages. A cantata, "We've Come from the City," written by Herbert Haufrecht, concerned the problems associated with the dam construction; it was performed first at Woodland and later at Carnegie Hall.[63]

In 1953, Woodland campers on a field trip discovered that Hurley, New York, was the birthplace of abolitionist and feminist Sojourner Truth. Not only did this lead to a camp presentation on the life and work of Sojourner Truth, but it led to the camp engaging in a campaign to have the site marked by a memorial statue. A Black woman sculptor worked on the design at the camp the next summer, but the campaign was, in the end, unsuccessful.[64]

In this interaction between urban and rural culture, by far the most important way in which Woodland attempted to create something new from it was in the area of folk music. The folk music of the Catskills offered Woodland organizers a cultural form that could be made the basis for a radical American culture. The three people primarily responsible for the camp's focus on folk songs and on the ways in which these songs were collected, transformed, and spread to a wider community, were Herbert Haufrecht, Norman Cazden, and Pete Seeger. Haufrecht was one of the founders of *People's Songs*, a magazine and an organization founded in the late 1940s to spread songs that were related to the left-wing movement. Norman Cazden was an academically trained musicologist and university professor who was later blacklisted after losing his job at the University of Illinois in 1953.[65]

Both Haufrecht and Cazden had been members of the Composers' Collective, a Communist-organized group founded in the early 1930s that included Marc Blitzstein, the creator of the English version of the Brecht/Weil Threepenny Opera, composers Aaron Copeland and Elie Seigmeister, and musicologist Charles Seeger—Pete Seeger's father.[66] It was in the Composers' Collective in the first years of the 1930s that radical, classically trained American musicians began to explore the use of folk songs to create a national and democratic music.[67] At the same time, New York radicals were being introduced to the political possibilities of rural folk music from Oklahoman Woody Guthrie and the veterans of the tenant farmer's struggles in Arkansas, Lee Hays and Agnes "Sis" Cunningham. Prior to this time, the music of the radical movement was, for the most part, hymnlike choral songs out of the European tradition. Radicals also identified with and listened to traditional music, both the ethnic folk songs of their own heritage and European classical music.

At Woodland, the new vision of folk music as popular, democratic culture was put into practice. It formed the framework for the cultural life of the camp. This process took three forms. In the first, traditional folk songs were collected, recorded, and put into musical notation by Haufrecht and Cazden—a process at first carried out without the use of tape recorders.[68] While the singer performed, a group of campers would copy the song's words and Haufrecht or Cazden would hurriedly transcribe the song in musical notation. A compilation of the songs collected by Cazden and Haufrecht over the years at Camp Woodland was published in 1982.[69] This effort was made in the spirit of preservation.

In a second part of the process, Haufrecht took the songs and stories of historical incidents gathered on camp excursions and turned them into musical pieces to be performed elsewhere. Thirdly, the camp emphasized the folk cultures of the diverse camp population. Both staff and campers were recruited under an active policy of maintaining an ethnically diverse group.

Pete Seeger was the person most centrally involved in bringing together the camp's diverse folk traditions. Already, in the 1940s, at the beginning his career, Seeger—who was to become the most prominent folk performer in the United States—took the songs from the variety of peoples represented at the camp and wove them into a perspective that was larger than the music itself. Because the folk music of different cultures could be sung on the same program, Seeger's ability to teach the songs and to put them in a radical political context was an important part of the process by which Camp Woodland was able to contribute to the making of a radical political culture that integrated international and interracial traditions. Seeger, for example, learned the song "Guantanamera" from a Cuban counselor at Woodland during summer 1961. He then recorded it and taught it to other singers, which spread the song around the world.[70] Seeger told a camper during a visit to Woodland, "Music is born out of the struggles of the people and it can only remain so long as it is mated to their struggles and hopes."[71]

Pete Seeger's visits to Woodland were special occasions for the camp, much in the way that the visits of prominent people to the other camps were. But his ties to Woodland were much stronger than, say, Robeson's had been to Wo-Chi-Ca. Seeger's in-laws were staff members at the camp from the 1940s through the mid-1950s and he himself became a music teacher at the Downtown Community School during the 1950s.[72]

Folk music was a vehicle for creating a culture at the camp during the summer, but it also could be taken back to the city during the school year. By combining the musical heritage of the Left with that of the rural Catskills and the multiethnic camp population, Woodland helped to create an alternative, radical culture. Like Kinderland's, its vision, involved ethnic pluralism; like Wo-Chi-Ca's it emphasized interracialism and manual labor; and it added a third component, the traditions of the rural community.

Woodland differed from Kinderland and Wo-Chi-Ca in important ways. It was not explicitly identified with a left-wing organization. It did, however, advertise in the *Daily Worker* and the *National Guardian* and scholarships to the camp were provided by the left-wing Drug Store Union, Local 1199 (now 1199, the National Health and Human Service Workers Union).[73]

Woodland also had a more middle-class constituency than the other two camps. Woodland's campers were not all from radical families, and the parents that were radicals often had professional jobs.[74] Furthermore, unlike Kinderland and Wo-Chi-Ca, political issues were notably absent from the camp yearbook. The camp newspaper, the *Catskill Caller*, written by campers, did take up political topics, however. For example, in 1949 the *Caller* included an article condemning the Smith Act trials and another that critically discussed loyalty oaths for teachers.[75]

The importance of the relationship between the camp and the people of the surrounding communities was also unique to Woodland. Both Kinderland and Wo-Chi-Ca were driven from their original homes because of hostility toward the camps by people living nearby. At Woodland, this did not occur because of Woodland's policy of building relationships with the people of the surrounding communities. At the end of the summer of 1955, Norman Studer was called to testify at the legislative committee investigating Communist influence in summer camps in New York. The day he was called was the same that was planned for the final camp banquet, at which camp members and community people gathered together for the last time of that summer. Everyone waited late into the evening for Studer to return. When he arrived, people from the communities around the camp spontaneously began to testify about the good the camp had done and what it had meant for them. The evening ended with everyone singing a song learned in the first years of the camp, "Friends and Neighbors":

> Friends and neighbors, I'm going to leave you.
> I have no doubt that you think it strange.
> But God be pleased, I never have rob-bed,
> Neither have I done any wrong.[76]

The belief at Woodland that the urban radical culture of the camp and the culture of the rural communities of the Catskills could find common ground may have had an effect: Woodland survived until 1961 and was closed for financial, not political reasons.[77]

CONCLUSION

Although different, each of the three camps discussed developed a program for children that attempted to respond to the crucial cultural issue facing American radicals during the 1930s and 1940s: how could radicals forge a cultural tradition and a vision of the future that addressed the problems of living in the United States? Each camp chose different aspects of American life they could emphasize and in which they could make a socialist intervention.

During this period, the Communist Party was addressing the same issue on a political rather than a cultural basis. The slogan "Communism is Twentieth Century Americanism," proclaimed by Communist leader Earl Browder, and the development of the policies of the Popular Front provided a political context for the organizers of the camps.

The culture or cultures created by Communists during the 1930s and 1940s were rooted in an attempt to join the Communist political perspective with the social and cultural concerns of the base of party members and sympathizers. It would be a mistake to view the activities of these camps solely as efforts to implement a "party line." In fact, the "party line" itself was often developed as a response to the groundswell of sympathy for radicalism that accompanied the Great Depression. The adoption by the Communist Party of a political strategy favorable to the movement of many Americans toward a radical analysis of American society allowed these social and educational experiments to take place within the Communist orbit. The relationship between the camp organizers and the Communist Party, I propose, was mutually informing. As children grew up in the camps, they took back to the Communist movement the cultural experiences and outlooks that were developed at camp. At the same time, the camps cannot be viewed separately from the history of the Communist Party itself. The identifications and allegiances of the organizers and staff members with the Communist Party was a grounding for the social and educational experimentation that they tried to provide for children during the summer.

Kinderland, Wo-Chi-Ca, and Woodland inhabited a world separate from, yet a part of, the Communist political movement. They were a part of the movement because the staff had political aims, and many of the children were drawn from families who had strong identification with the Communist Party. Yet the camp experience was also a separate part of the radical world, even in the city. Workers and children from the camps maintained friendships over the winter, and some organized activities in the city were carried out by camp alumni. In this way the utopian aspect of camp life was continued. Summer was a time during which children could leave the world of capitalism to live in a community that reflected the values of the radical movement, diverse though they were. The experience touched many of them profoundly and gave them a vision they could carry with them through their lives. As the Wo-Chi-Ca *Yearbook* described the goals of that camp:

> *Wo-Chi-Ca is the comradeship of children,*
> *An Inspiration for a world our own,*
> *Where noisy laughter has a peaceful echo,*
> *Giving courage to a future we will own.*[78]

primers for revolution

Communist Books for Children

During the 1930s, writers sympathetic to the Communist Party
created an enormous body of literature for adults. The period's novels,
short stories, poems, and plays have been the subject of extensive discussion by historians and literary critics; indeed, the development of "proletarian literature" under the aegis of the Communist Party through journals such as the *New Masses* and *Anvil* is considered one of the most
striking aspects of the decade's literary creation.

Similar efforts in the field of children's and young adult literature
have received virtually no attention.[1] In fact, only the English author
Geoffrey Trease, who, after writing a number of radical historical novels for young people, went on to become prominent as an author of
more mainstream fiction for young adults, is mentioned in the standard
work in the field of children's literature—and even then, Trease's radical novels from the early 1930s are ignored.[2] The lack of attention paid
to radical children's literature seems to reflect the neglect of children's
political activities in general.

Between 1925 and 1950, almost forty books whose characters, plots,
and settings reflected the outlook of the Communist Party were published—most of them by International Publishers, the CP publishing
house, but a few by the Young Pioneers of America, the IWO, other
allied organizations, and individual authors.[3] These books reflected the
political culture of the Communist Party during the 1920s, 1930s, and
1940s. They were written and published for use by the Young Pioneers

and the IWO Juniors. In the summer camps they were distributed through the network of Communist bookstores and organizations.[4] Both the form and content varied widely: the books included fairy tales for young children, novels for adolescents, science books, a song book, and a collection of plays. Most of the forty books in this study were the work of American authors, but two were first published in German, two in Russian, and at least four first appeared in England.[5]

Max Bedacht, general secretary of the IWO, described the purpose of these books in his introduction to the *New Pioneer Story Book,* a compilation of stories that had first appeared in the *New Pioneer* magazine. He emphasized that the stories in the book would help children gain a greater understanding of the world around them, and thus, in standard Marxist reasoning, increase their ability to change that world. He directly addressed young readers:

> What you are learning in school now and what you read outside of school, in newspapers and books and magazines, is determining what you will do when you grow up. The rich people who own this country know that. That is why they want the government to control education. These rich men, the capitalists, also control the literature you read. American literature is rich in children's books and stories and magazines. But these books were not written to give you pleasure. They are written in order to give you certain ideas that the rich men want you to have. . . . Reading these stories will help you understand the life about you. As you learn to understand life you will learn to shape your own lives. You will not merely be pawns kicked around by destiny; you will become masters of your own destiny. You will not only be part of history, but you will become makers of history.[6]

The Communist approach to children's education and political socialization made itself felt in radical children's books. Children were encouraged to participate in the political activities of the revolutionary movement. During the early 1930s, the belief that children needed to engage in political activity autonomously from their parents was an important aspect of the children's books. The books published during the Popular Front period focused on the relationship between children and the labor movement, and on "progressive" re-tellings of incidents in U.S. history.

The complex relationship between the culture of the Communist

movement and the diverse ethnic cultures in the United States and elsewhere played an important thematic role in many of the stories in all
periods. Although characters from European immigrant backgrounds
are rare in this literature until the late 1930s, minority characters were
present in greater numbers than in any other children's literature in the
United States until the impact of the civil rights movement during the
1960s.

Almost every collection of stories contained at least one in which
Black characters, or at least one Black character, were prominent. The
first collection of children's stories published by the Communist Party
in the United States, *Fairy Tales for Workers' Children* (1925), included a
story about a Black child's escape from slavery in the South. Two stories
in *Battle in the Barnyard* (1932) concern Black children, as does one in
the *New Pioneer Story Book* (1935). American Indian and Hispanic
characters were also present. The international setting of many stories
provided readers with sympathetic characters drawn from countries
and cultures vastly different from white America: Latin Americans in
Call to Arms (1935) and "Julio Fights, Too" in the *New Pioneer Story
Book;* Gypsies in *Eddie and the Gypsy* (1935); Japanese in "Reddening the
Sky," a story in *Martin's Annual* (1935).

Communists were not the first to try to teach oppositional values
through children's literature. In 1842, Black Garrisonian abolitionists
published *Anti-Slavery Offering and Picknick,* a book, and the *Slave's
Friend,* a children's magazine.[7] In 1859, the Sunday School Union published *The Child's Anti-Slavery Book,* a collection of stories meant to
inculcate abolitionist sentiments in children.[8] During the first decades
of the twentieth century, authors affiliated with the Socialist Party of
America wrote books for use in the Socialist Sunday schools. Nicholas
Klein's *The Socialist Primer* (1908), John Spargo's *Socialist Readings for
Children* (1909), Caroline Nelson's *Nature Talks on Economics* (1912),
and Mary E. Marcy's *Stories of the Cave People* (1917) and *Rhymes of
Early Jungle Folk* (1922) were written explicitly to inculcate socialist
ideas. A six-book series, *Industrial and Social History,* written by Dewey
student Elizabeth Doop, was used to teach the general processes of
social evolution.[9]

Kenneth Teitelbaum has found that Klein's, Spargo's, and Nelson's
books were recommended in the socialist press for use in Socialist
Sunday schools and that they formed part of the curriculum in several

such Sunday schools in New York, Milwaukee, Newport, and San Francisco.[10] Although *The Socialist Primer* gives only simple definitions for words like "boss," "worker," and "socialism," the other four books include stories with more complex explanations of the socialist worldview.

In the Socialist children's books, science, especially Darwinism and evolutionary theory, play an important role. This reflects the perspective, common in the socialist movement at that time, that the scientific theories of biological evolution supported the socialist belief for the necessity of social evolution. In his recent *American Socialists and Evolutionary Thought, 1870–1920,* Mark Pittenger traces how important to American socialists prior to the First World War was the perception that Darwin's theories supported Marxist analysis. He shows that the Socialist belief in this connection transcended the political divisions within the Socialist Party, even while different tendencies attempted to use Darwinism to support differing political and strategic analyses.[11]

Nelson, Marcy, and Spargo all shared the view that biological evolution implies the necessity of social evolution. Their differences in emphasis, however, reflect their different stands in the period's internal Socialist Party debates. Both Nelson and Marcy were sympathetic to the Industrial Workers of the World, which placed them to the left.[12] In Nelson's stories, the points at which changes occur in the natural world are marked by a significant rupturing in the natural microcosm; for example, the baby bird breaks through the walls of the egg when it is time for it to be born. Marcy, too, saw conflict as a moving force in evolution: her early humans struggle against nature for mastery, as well as among themselves in early manifestations of social conflict. Spargo, on the other hand, was a right-wing Socialist who would leave socialism behind by the 1920s. For him, the transition from capitalism to socialism would be a gradual and inevitable process, occurring in much the same way as in his view of biological evolution.

In Nelson's *Nature Talks on Economics*, the relationship between the natural and the social world is at the center of the book's argument. The book is organized around discussions between two children and their mother and carpenter father. In "Evolution and Revolution," one of her chapters, the children ask how birds grow inside eggs. The change from egg to bird is described in a political metaphor:

There was a revolt against living any longer in the egg-state. It meant death and starvation. "Strike down the wall!" was the cry. And the bird did something he had never done before; he moved his head and struck blow after blow.

"Then he came out," said Johnnie with glee.

"Yes, he came out," said his father, "because he didn't remain quiet and say—'It is no use. I have always been an egg and therefore always shall be an egg until I die.' All life has come up from a mere speck, and labored mightily until it was so changed that it had to find a new way of living. This laboring mightily is evolution.

"The cry, 'Strike down the wall!' is the cry of revolution."

From this explanation of the workings of the natural world, an explanation of the social world soon follows:

The working class is in a shell of Capitalism. What they have built, a few idle rich claim as their private property. Every day the workers have less and less food. . . . Strike down the wall of capitalism is our cry. We must have food or die. And we shall not die while we produce food in plenty.[13]

"The Crystal Builders" uses the construction of crystals in nature to illustrate further points about social evolution. Fractures in a mineral crystal are explained as the result of a conflict between crystals at different temperatures. The father connects this feature of crystal building to what occurs in society: "Nearly all fights can be traced to the struggle for possessions [sic] of a nice warm corner of life."[14]

Mary Marcy similarly used "natural history" as a way of drawing lessons about social and political history. In her introduction to *Stories of the Cave People,* she explains her view that stories about evolution and the lives of early human beings contribute to a radical outlook. First, she saw her work as an attack on religious superstition, a critique of those who credited a supernatural agency with humanity's progress from "lowest savagery" to civilization. Second, she argues that the only "stable fact in the world to-day is the process of change."[15] Like many Socialists, she saw the relationship between evolution and socialism to be the fact the road to socialist consciousness was through the rational and scientific understanding of the world. Marcy wrote: "No man or woman can begin to intelligently interpret the causes of social phenomena and human progress to-day without a practical knowledge of sociology and a general understanding of the underlying causes of social evolution."[16]

In *Socialist Readings for Children,* Spargo uses biological arguments to buttress his gradualist analysis of social change. In "A Little Talk on Evolution," the children, who are the main characters, have been reading a book about socialism. They ask the mother to explain the use of the term *evolution.* She replies:

> You remember, that the Socialist knows that he can trust the law of evolution to bring change. . . . So what the writer of the book meant was that the Socialist knows that evolution will bring the change to Socialism; that we shall grow to it. If you see a tadpole in the water you saw that it will change and become a frog, that evolution will change it. And the wise men have found out that the ways in which people live in the world—their laws, their customs, their governments change in just the same way. So they say that the manner in which we live is the result of evolution.[17]

Regardless of their differences, the importance of biological evolution in the works of these three authors highlights the importance of Darwinian theory in the worldview of Socialists before the First World War. By comparison, its absence from Communist children's books is notable. The Communist emphasis on voluntary action and participation in political struggle distinguishes their children's stories from the Socialist tales of natural and inevitable change.

But one Communist children's book's emphasis on the relationship between biological and social evolution was similar to that of the Socialists. This was *Science and History for Boys and Girls* (1932), written and published by William Montgomery Brown. Brown had been the Episcopal bishop of Arkansas when he lost his faith in the existence of God and was expelled from the Episcopal Council of Bishops in 1925. He had become a Communist early in the 1920s, and over the course of the decade he published a number of books and pamphlets. For the most part, these dealt with his conflict with the Episcopal Church, justifying his position.[18]

Science and History for Boys and Girls was his only book for children. Written for those of twelve years and older, it is more than three hundred pages long and covers the entire history of life on earth from a Darwinian/Marxist perspective. Richard Levins, the Marxist agronomist, recalled in his article "A Science of Our Own: Marxism and Nature" that he was introduced to the link between science and history when his grandfather read to him from Bishop Brown's book when he was a child.[19] The first part of the book is devoted to an evolutionary treatment of nature: the growth and evolution of animals, the creation of the universe, and the early evolution of human beings. Much of it would be rather commonplace today, except for the frequent jibes at church fathers and superstitious believers who denied the scientific basis of evolution and wanted the teaching of evolution banned from schools. After accounting for the evolution of human beings, Brown gives a Marxist analysis of the evolution of society from primitive tribe to capitalist trust. As in the earlier section, he pays special attention to the role of religious leaders in masking exploitation. For Brown, as for the socialists, theories of biological and social evolution are the basis for belief in the inevitability of socialism:

> There is going to be a very wonderful life on this earth for all men, women and children. And science tells us that it is going to last for millions of years, perhaps more than a hundred million years.
>
> So we must all help to get that wonderful life started as soon as possible, and then science will make the world richer and richer and everybody will get his or her share.[20]

However, in general, Socialist children's books differed from those of the Communists. The themes of children's involvement in politics, the importance of ethnic diversity, the experience by children of economic injustice, and conflictual relations within the family are all absent in the Socialist children's books, while they form the core of those books published under the auspices of the Communist Party.

The children in both *Nature Talks on Economics* and *Socialist Readings for Children* do not suffer from living under capitalism. Indeed, the family portrayed in Nelson's book is that of a skilled craftsman; the family in Spargo's book is that of a wealthy Socialist intellectual. Most significantly, while these books were intended to guide children toward socialism, activism in the socialist cause is for adults only. As John Spargo wrote in the socialist "catechism" concluding his book, "Boys and girls cannot do very much until they grow older . . . when they are men and women they will be able to take the places of the men and women who are doing all the hard work for the cause now."[21]

The first children's book published by the Communist Party was *Fairy Tales for Workers Children* (1925) by Herminia zur Mühlen. Published originally in German, the book contains four fables with revolutionary morals. The first story, "The Rose Bush," concerns the evils of private property and the right of workers to the proceeds of their labor. A rosebush speaks to the gardener who tends her and offers him some of her flowers. He refuses, explaining that the flowers belong to the woman who employs him. The rosebush is horrified and protests that, in the natural world, each gets the benefits of what he or she produces. In her disbelief, she asks the wind whether what the gardener has told her is true. The wind affirms that it is. The rosebush decides to refuse to bloom for the rich anymore. When the wealthy lady comes to pick her flowers, the rosebush pricks her with thorns. Finally, she refuses all water until she dries up and is thrown out. The gardener can then take her home, where she blooms once more to bring cheer to the poor.

In "The Little Grey Dog," a small dog helps a Black slave, a boy, to escape from a sugar plantation in the South. As they are escaping, the overseer catches the dog and kills him, which allows Benjamin, the slave boy, to escape northward. In both "Sparrow" and "Why?" figures from nature answer children's questions about why there is so much poverty and exploitation in the world. All the stories look toward a future in which workers will have united and overthrown their exploiters.

The fairy-tale form of the stories in *Fairy Tales for Workers' Children* reflects their German origin. When Mike Gold reviewed the book for the Communist *Workers' Monthly* in 1925, he criticized what he called the stories' "atmosphere of slave wistfulness, depression and yearning," arguing that "the proletariat must grow away from the mood of Christian slave-revolt" traditionally reflected in the fairy-tale form. Instead, Gold said, children's stories should reflect truly proletarian ideology by showing the real conditions of real workers.[22]

The books written by American authors contained more realistic stories, in line with Gold's proposals, as well as fables and fairy tales. *Battle in the Barnyard* (1932) by Helen Kay was written as a sequel to *Fairy Tales for Workers' Children,* and like zur Mühlen's book it was directed at younger children. The stories in *Battle in the Barnyard* concern children's responses to the Great Depression. The first, "Bread," begins:

Jane put her head on the desk. It felt heavy and dull. She was weak and sick. Her stomach was empty. It seemed to gnaw and cry, "Please put some bread and butter into me. If you don't I'll keep being empty and I'll gnaw and gnaw, and make your head ache until you do."[23]

Jane is told by her teacher to leave school until she can concentrate on her lessons. On her way home, feeling dejected as well as hungry, she meets her friend Cora. Cora brings her to a Young Pioneer demonstration. The Pioneers are picketing the school demanding free lunches for the children of the unemployed. In the demonstration Jane is arrested, but she is no longer despondent because she knows that the solution to her problems lies in struggle.

"Strike Secret" in *Battle in the Barnyard* is similar to "Bread" in that it presents children confronted with social conflict. Johnnie is a miner's son. His friends accuse him of being the son of a scab and Johnnie fights to defend his father's reputation. He returns home feeling ashamed and humiliated and asks his father whether it is true that he went to work that day. His father affirms that he did go into the mine, and Johnnie, ashamed, runs away to the woods. When his father comes to find him, he explains that he is working for the union, trying to get working miners to join the strike. This is a secret that Johnnie must tell no one. The next day, Johnnie is expelled from his gang, but he doesn't let on that his father is really not a scab. When the strike is over, Johnnie explains to his friends that his father was working for the union.

Black children are the subjects of two of the stories in *Battle in the Barnyard*. In "Us Alley Kids," Willie, a Black child living in the South, climbs over a wall into the garden of a large estate. The weather is very hot and Willie wants to cool himself in the shade of the trees in the garden. He is chased out by the groundskeeper and the owners, who tell him that because he is poor and Black he has no right to enjoy the garden. In "A Night's Adventure," a group of four Black and four white Young Pioneers are distributing leaflets at night in Washington, D.C. The adventure of the title occurs when a group of them go into a Black church and hand out leaflets to the congregation over the objections of the preacher.

While African American characters are present to a remarkable degree for children's literature of the time, prior to the mid-1930s few of the white characters have any identifiable ethnic background. The lack of recognition of ethnic differences among whites in these children's books is particularly noticeable in light of the largely immigrant base of the Communist Party during the 1920s and 1930s. The Young Pioneer and IWO Junior readers of these stories were very likely to be immigrants themselves, or children of immigrants. This lack is a distinguishing characteristic between the Communist children's literature and the radical adult literature of the same period. In fact, the only discussion of distinctions among European ethnic groups occurred in books first published in Europe, where the effort to overcome hostility between different nationalities occupied the same place in the thinking of European Communist parties as did the effort to overcome racial animosity in the United States.

The reason for this neglect of the immigrant experience in the Communist children's literature was that the Communist Party wanted to expand its influence beyond the radical ethnic communities. It attempted to organize in industries and regions with a nonimmigrant working class. Two of the party's most successful efforts in this regard before the mid-1930s were in the Gastonia, North Carolina, textile strike of 1929 and the organization of the National Miners' Union in the late 1920s and early 1930s. In both these situations, most of the workers involved were native-born Americans, not immigrants.[24] Both strikes were represented in the children's books of the period because of their importance in Communist political strategy to reach out to these workers. "Pickets and Slippery Sticks" by Myra Page, in the *New Pioneer Story Book*, is set in a Gastonia-type Southern textile town[25]; "Strike Secret" in Kay's *Battle in the Barnyard* deals with the struggle in the coal mines.

After 1936, the focus on native-born workers, and the neglect in children's books of the ethnic dimension of American culture, changed. Influenced by the change in Communist policy toward that of the Popular Front against Fascism, Communist children's literature came to reflect new forms of political culture. For example, there was far greater expression of ethnicity among white Americans, along with the continuing presence of African Americans. In the collection of stories entitled *Corky: Adventure Stories for Young People* (1938) by Eric Lucas, "The Battle of Black Hole Dock" is about the conflict between Jewish and Irish youth gangs over a swimming dock on the river. At the same time, Communist authors continued to look for examples of working-class struggle outside of the immigrant communities, now portraying

events and figures from American history and culture in a more posi-
tive light. Thus in *Corky* there is "Buckhorn Valley Tales," purportedly
based on Abraham Lincoln's youth, and "Swamp Fox," which features
guerrilla soldiers during the American Revolution. The latter story was
expanded by Lucas into a full-length historical novel for young people,
The Swamp Fox Brigade (1945).

The attempt by the Communists to relate to the American tradition
was further expanded by the Mid-western Communist writer Meridel
Le Sueur, who wrote four children's books with themes drawn from the
American tradition in the period following the Second World War: *Little
Brother of the Wilderness: The Story of Johnny Appleseed (1947), Nancy
Hanks of Wilderness Road: A story of Abraham Lincoln's Mother (1949),
Sparrow Hawk (1950), and Chanticleer of Wilderness Road: A Story of Davy
Crockett* (1951). In 1946, International published an edition of the poetry
of Walt Whitman, with an introduction written by Langston Hughes.

The relationship between children and adults presented in the stories
was another change after 1936. Adults had never been entirely absent
from the earlier stories, but their role had been ambiguous. Where
adults were present, negative characterizations were common. Often,
children were presented as learning radical politics from other children
or on their own. By the late 1930s, parents and other adults figure prominently as the sources of radical understanding among children. In "Salty
Steers His Course" and "Rusty," both in *Corky*, the main character is
drawn into political struggle by his father's union activities. In Jean
Karsavina's *Reunion in Poland* (1945), a young woman returns with her
father to Poland after the Second World War, having spent the war years
in exile in Moscow. Her loyalty to her father's beliefs is what gives her
the strength to confront her mother's death at the hands of the Nazis and
to search for her adopted brother, an anti-Nazi partisan.

The incorporation of children into the labor and revolutionary
movements was central to all the books for children published by the
Communists. During the 1930s, these were presented for younger
readers in the *New Pioneer Story Book, Corky,* and *Who Are the Young
Pioneers?* (1934). Longer novels for older children and adolescents, such
as the historical novels by Geoffrey Trease, were also published during
the 1930s.

"Siksika," the first story in the *New Pioneer Story Book,* concerns
American Indians. Good Man is an Indian worker in a salmon cannery

in the Pacific Northwest. He is fired for his militance during a strike. The employers attempt to frame him on a murder charge and he is killed by white vigilantes who go to his village to find him. Before he dies, Good Man explains to his two children, Black Hair and Lone Star, how the Indian people are exploited by the capitalists who own the canneries, and that his plight, rather than being an issue of whites versus Indians, is a conflict between all workers and their bosses. His last words are to tell his children to carry on the struggle. Although the point of this story seems to be that Indians are no longer the people of a romanticized West, and no longer "primitives," some aspects of the story read like a movie western. The Indians call automobiles "fire wagons" and liquor is referred to as "fire water."

In "Don't Cry over Spilt Milk," also in the *New Pioneer Story Book,* Ann and Paul are farmers' children during the time of a farmers' milk strike. Left alone at home while their father and mother are on the picket line, they confront state troopers who are collecting milk from the striking farmers in order to break the strike. The children hide the milk at their farm and also warn their neighbors. At the end of the story, the two children join their parents in singing "Solidarity" at the mass meeting of farmers. This story is one of the few in which an intact family is positively portrayed..

Myra Page's "Pickets and Slippery Sticks," another tale in the New Pioneer collection, is set in a Southern textile town. Page, who edited the *Young Pioneer* for part of the 1920s, also wrote two well-known adult novels: *Gathering Storm* (1932) about the Gastonia textile strike, and *With Sun in Our Blood* (1950), about coal miners. "Pickets and Slippery Sticks" shows how a friendship between two Black and two white children is broken up due to the racism of the white parents. The white parents learn to overcome their racism during a strike in the mill where they all work, and the children reactivate their friendship.

Other stories in the *New Pioneer Story Book* include "The Journal of a German Pioneer," in which the son of anti-Fascists helps organize other children against the Nazis, "Bloody Sunday," about a child in the Russian Revolution of 1905, and "Song of the Eagle," in which children join the Unemployed Councils in resisting evictions. In each of these stories, children are presented as activists in their own right, joining adults in a common cause.

Who Are the Young Pioneers? was written as a recruiting pamphlet for the Young Pioneers of America. It contains vignettes of Young Pioneer activity in many parts of the country, including that of the children of steel workers, miners, and sharecroppers, as well as of child workers. The author, Martha Campion, claimed in her preface that all the stories were true. Leslie, the son of sharecroppers in the South, helps in the organization of the sharecroppers' union.[26] When the sharecroppers have a union meeting, it is Leslie and his fellow Pioneers who are the guards, watching the roads and paths; they warn the "croppers if they hear horses hoofs [sic] or the motor of a car or other such sign that the sheriff or the Ku Klux have found out about the meeting and are on their way to break it up or shoot it up."[27]

The stories in *Corky* (1938) are similar in their presentation of children's political development to those of the earlier books, except that they represent the outlook of the Communist Party during the Popular Front era of the late 1930s. Thus there is less overtly Marxist discussion. The political outlook of the stories represents the Communist Party's stated commitment to the preservation and extension of democracy. For example: In "Salty Steers His Course," Salty works on a fishing boat with his father, Pop, who has been organizing other working fishermen to get higher prices from Balfour, the man who controls the fish market. To combat the fishermen's organization, Balfour has organized the Crawfish Vigilantes, a strong-arm squad. After Pop is beaten up, Salty discovers where the Crawfish Vigilantes are having a secret meeting. He gathers the other fishermen and they march on the meeting and unmask the leaders—Balfour and the sheriff. No longer afraid of the 'vigilantes, the fishermen learn the value of unity and organization. In "Salty," a more general working-class and labor unity has replaced the explicit explication of how socialism is necessary if the problems of the workers are to be solved.

In the novels for older children, the themes of working-class solidarity, the importance of overcoming ethnic divisions, and the necessity of political struggle to achieve justice again are stressed. These books have more complex story lines and the characters in them are more developed than in the books for younger children. Examples of these are Trease's *Call to Arms,* Alex Wedding's *Eddie and the Gypsy,* and *Tree by the Waters,* (1948) by Jean Karsavina. Of these three authors, only Karsavina was American, but all three books were published by the American Communist Party.

Call to Arms is a novel of revolution in Central America. It is set in a fictional country, Coravia, that looks remarkably like Nicaragua.[28] The story begins with international arms merchants stirring up a war between Coravia and the neighboring Vacquil. At the same time, Nita, a girl from the slums, gets involved in the revolutionary movement. Her friends Pedro and Ramon are swept up in the tide of "patriotic" fervor and both join the army, but the war disillusions both boys. Pedro is shot for agitating against the war in the army; Ramon escapes and finds his way back to the city. He again meets up with Nita, who brings him into the revolutionary movement. Together they participate in the rebellion that topples the reactionary government. The novel ends with a celebration of the new soviet government of Coravia, complete with marching workers and hammer-and-sickle flags.

Eddie and the Gypsy was published first in German. Eddie is the son of a Berlin worker during the 1920s. Although his father had scabbed during a recent strike at his factory, he had nonetheless been laid off. Eddie's two friends are Max Kablunde, whose parents are Communists, and Unku, a Gypsy girl he meets at a fair. The story involves Eddie's adventures as he tries to help his family while his father is unemployed. Max's mother helps him to get a job as a delivery boy and Unku lends him money to make a down payment on a bicycle. The main dramatic contrasts in the novel are between Eddie's family and those of Max and Unku. Eddie's father, lacking class consciousness, takes out his frustration on his family and on himself. The members of Max's family, which is as poor as Eddie's (his father has been blacklisted), are hopeful because their political beliefs give them confidence in the future. The members of Unku's family, like Eddie's father, lack class consciousness, but they have a naive solidarity with others who are suffering. There is a warmth in the two families that is lacking in Eddie's. The story climaxes during a strike. While Eddie's father gets a job as a scab, Max's father is forced to hide from the police because of his role as a strike leader. Eddie turns off his father's alarm clock to stop him getting to the factory on time. That same day, scabs riding in the car that was to have taken Eddie's father to work are beaten by strikers, and Eddie's father, grateful at having escaped the beating, agrees to hide Max's father from the police. As the story ends, Unku invites Eddie to accompany her family to the countryside that summer.

The political themes of *Eddie and the Gypsy* are those of most stories published by Communists during this period. In many particulars, the book reflects the concerns of the German Communist Party during the latter part of the 1920s. The connection between Eddie's father's lack of class consciousness and his harshness toward his family, and the belief in the "natural" solidarity of Gypsies, marks this book as European in origin.

In *Tree by the Waters,* Abby Chapin is a young factory worker in a New England mill town during the 1930s. Although Abby is connected through family ties and ethnic identification to the factory owners and the rest of the upper class of her town, class differences create a wide gulf between them. Her boyfriend is the son of the manager of the factory where she works. The story revolves around Abby's efforts to understand the relationships between ethnic identification and class identification. When the workers in the factory go on strike, she realizes that she will have to choose between her Yankee friends and the Polish American women who are her fellow workers. She discovers that the ties of class transcend the ties of ethnicity and that solidarity among workers is more important than the concerns of her personal life.[29]

Historical settings were often used to teach the lessons of the importance of class solidarity, struggle against oppression, and the overcoming of ethnic differences. Like the presentation of history in mainstream children's books, the history presented in radical children's literature was used primarily for its moral lessons.

In the two historical novels for young people written by Geoffrey Trease, *Bows Against the Barons* (1934) and *Comrades for the Charter* (1934), radical political themes are presented in an English historical setting. *Bows Against the Barons* is a re-telling of the story of Robin Hood in radical terms. In the traditional story, Robin Hood is loyal to the "true" King Richard, and is waiting for him to return from the Crusades. In Trease's version, Robin espouses the hope of a future kingdom of equality for all that will be the result of the successful struggle of the peasantry against the nobles.

Comrades for the Charter is set in the 1830s during the great Chartist agitation in Britain. A Welsh boy, Owen, and an English boy, Tom, meet while they are wandering the Welsh countryside looking for work. They are employed by a Chartist agitator masquerading as a patent medicine salesman. He draws both boys into the work of organizing for the Charter. Among the issues that form a backdrop to the story are the struggle to overcome Welsh-English ethnic antagonism, and the ways that coal mining is beginning to destroy the natural beauty of the Welsh countryside.

The moral lessons of history were also taught in stories for younger children. *Our Lenin* by Ruth Shaw and Harry Alan Potamkin is an illustrated biography of Lenin for younger children. The story of the Russian Revolution, and Lenin's role in it, is told in a simplified manner, with the authors emphasizing the "great love" that working people all over the world have for Lenin. In the *Red Corner Book* (c.1932), a collection of stories, poems, and activities originally published in England, there are stories about the French Revolution of 1789, the English Peasant Uprising of 1391, the Paris Commune, the Irish revolutionary, James Connolly, and the Russian Revolution.

Beginning in 1925 Communist children's literature represented a highly politicized view of children's education and socialization. In all the stories, whether for young children or adolescents, the values of working-class solidarity, and participation in the working-class movement are the central themes..

After the Second World War, International Publishers returned to the themes of science and nature that had been so prevalent in the Socialist children's books. Unlike the earlier children's books published by International, and even the books published by the Socialists, politics were almost entirely absent from this series. In *Egg to Chick* (1946) by Millicent E. Selsam and From *Head to Foot: Our Bodies and How They Work* (1946) by Alex Novikoff, for example, the authors make no effort to connect scientific explanations to social analysis. This apparent de-politicization of children's books reflects Communist expectations in the postwar period they would be accepted as a legitimate part of the American political landscape. The transformation of the Communist Party into the Communist Political Association in 1944, and the CPA's subsequent rejection of revolutionary goals were expressions of these hopes.

The Communist children's and young adult books expressed the perspective that informed the organization of children's activities. As the activities changed, the literature reflected those changes. In the children's books published between 1925 and 1934, children were encouraged to participate in the political activities of the Communist movement on their own. This outlook reflected an autonomous Communist political culture, separate from the cultures both of the immigrant workers who made up the Communist Party and of the mainstream culture of the United States. By the mid-1930s this began to change as the Communist political culture came to express the ways in which Communists grappled with coming to terms with both ethnic and native-born culture, in order to form a radical alternative within, rather than separate from American culture in general.

APPENDIX
Radical Children's Books: A Bibliography

Of the forty-five books listed, forty-three are English-language works that were published in the United States. The three other titles appear at the end of the list. One is in Finnish and two were published in England, not the United States.

Adler, Irving. *The Secret of Light.* New York: International Publishers, 1952. Part of the Young World Series, dealing mainly with scientific subjects, published by International Publishers beginning in the late 1940s.

Blake, Ben. *Twelve Plays for Boys and Girls.* New York: Federation of Children's Organizations and the Junior Section of the International Workers' Order, 1935. Plays for use by left-wing children's organizations. Includes works taken from *Fairy Tales for Workers' Children* as well as plays about the Paris Commune and the Russian Revolution.

Beauchamp, Joan. *Martin's Annual.* New York: International Publishers, 1935. A collection of stories, pictures, and games that was simultaneously copublished in London by Martin Lawrence, Ltd. It includes, among other things, a number of stories by Geoffrey Trease, a cooking lesson for children, a Communist ABC, and instructions on how to build a model theater.

Bobinska, Helena, and Kasimir Hertel. *The Revenge of the Kabanauri.* New York: International Publishers, 1935. Translated from Russian, this is a story of a foundling child growing up amid the Russian Civil War of 1919–1922 in Tiflis, Georgia.

Brown, William Montgomery. *Science and History for Boys and Girls.* Galion, OH: Bradford-Brown Publishing, 1932. A history of the world from the time of creation, through human evolution to modern society and beyond. From a Darwinian/Marxist perspective. By the former Episcopal bishop of Arkansas.

Campion, Martha. *New Pioneer Story Book.* New York: New Pioneer Publishing,

1935. A collection of stories most of which were first published in the *New Pioneer* magazine. Deals with children's relationships to the radical movement.

————. *Who Are the Young Pioneers?*. New Pioneer Publishing, 1934. Vignettes, purportedly true, about the activities of members of the Young Pioneers of America. Set in the United States and other countries.

Davidman, Solomon. *Jewish Children in Biro-Bidjan*. Brooklyn, NY: Published by the author, 1948. Bilingual Yiddish-English collection of stories written between 1932 and 1945. Yiddish short-story writer Davidman was also a teacher in the shules of the International Workers' Order. The stories all concern children in Biro-Bidjan, the Jewish autonomous region of the Soviet Union.

Hollos, Clara. *The Story of Your Coat*. New York: International Publishers, 1946. The story of how a coat is made, from the people who tend the sheep to the people who sew the coat. Part of the Young World Series.

————. *The Story of Your Bread*. New York: International Publishers, 1948. From wheat to bakery—the story of bread.

Ilin, M. *How the Automobile Learned to Run*. New York: International Publishers, 1945. A history of the automobile.

————. *Giant at the Crossroads: The Story of Ancient Civilization*. New York: International Publishers, 1948. A Marxist treatment of the civilizations of Egypt, Greece, and Rome. Part of the Young World Series.

IWO National Pioneer Council. *Poems and Recitations for Workers' Children*. New York: International Workers' Order, n.d. but ca. 1930. Not available.

Kay, Helen. *Battle in the Barnyard*. New York: Workers Library Publishers, 1932. A collection of stories for young children. The main theme is how children come to understand the true workings of capitalism and learn to fight for socialism.

Klein, Nicholas. *The Socialist Primer*. Girard, Kansas: Appeal to Reason, 1908. Organized into a series of lessons, the book uses simple words to explain the evils of capitalism and the benefits of socialism. This is the only piece of literature directed toward children to come out of the large Socialist movement of Oklahoma and Kansas that was served by the *Appeal to Reason* newspaper.

Karsavina, Jean. *Reunion in Poland*. New York: International Publishers, 1945. The story of a Polish girl who after exile in Moscow with her father during the Second World War returns to Poland to help build socialism and perhaps find her mother and adopted brother. Her mother, she learns, has been killed by the Nazis, but she finds her brother, a partisan. Illustrated by well-known artist Lynd Ward.

————. *Tree by the Waters*. New York: International Publishers, 1948. Story about a Yankee girl during the late 1930s in a New England factory town made up of Yankees and Polish Americans. When there is a strike, she has to contend with ethnic and class divisions in the town and comes to realize she has more

in common with her Polish American fellow-workers than with the Yankee
bosses and their families with whom she has socialized.

Le Sueur, Meridel. *Little Brother of the Wilderness: The Story of Johnny Appleseed.*
Illus. Betty Alder. New York: Knopf, 1947.

————. *Nancy Hanks of Wilderness Road: A Story of Abraham Lincoln's Mother.*
New York: Knopf, 1949.

————. *Sparrow Hawk.* Illus. William Mayes. New York: Knopf, 1950.

————. *Chanticleer of Wilderness Road.* Illus. Alden Watson. New York: Knopf,
1951.

Lucas, Eric. *Corky: Adventure Stories for Young People.* New York: International
Publishers, 1938. Some of the stories are about children involved in strikes;
others are set in American history and present the viewpoint of the
Communist Party during the Popular Front period.

————. *Swamp Fox Brigade.* New York: International Publishers, 1945. A historical novel for adolescents about guerrilla soldiers during the American
Revolution. Presents the viewpoint that the small farmers who fought in the
Revolution believed in the kind of radical democracy being emphasized by
the Communist Party during the late 1930s and the 1940s.

————. *Voyage Thirteen.* New York: International Publishers, 1946. Two boys
ship out on one of the last merchant ships carrying Lend-Lease to Europe
after the Second World War. The crew, which includes a Black cook, a
Spanish anti-Fascist veteran of the Spanish Civil War, and an old-time sailor
who remembers the days of the clipper ships, teach the boys about class consciousness, the importance of trade unions, and the necessity of overcoming
ethnic and racial prejudice.

Marcy, Mary E. *Rhymes of Early Jungle Folk.* Woodcuts by Wharton H. Eshrick.
Chicago: Charles H. Kerr, 1922. Poems for children on the themes of evolution
and the life of early human beings. Emphasizes the inevitable processes of social
change and the interdependence of humans and the natural world. Contains
something of a view of what primitive communism would have looked like.
The poems are saved from an overly romantic perspective by a Marxist focus on
hardships caused by ignorance and the inevitability of social conflict. Marcy was
an editor of the left-wing Socialist *International Socialist Review*.

————. *Stories of the Cave People.* Chicago: Charles H. Kerr, 1917. Marcy writes
in her introduction, "In this little book I have sought . . . to present only the
first steps in human progress as elaborated by Lewis Henry Morgan." Similar
to her later *Rhymes,* described above.

Mühlen, Herminia zur. *Fairy Tales for Workers' Children.* Trans. Ida Dailes.
Chicago: Daily Worker Publishing, 1925. The first children's book published
by the Communist Party in the United States. It was written originally in
German. Contains four "fairy tales" teaching the importance of class con-

sciousness and solidarity. The author also wrote *Little Allies* (London: Alliance Press, ca. 1944) while in exile from Germany.

Nelson, Caroline. *Nature Talks on Economics.* Chicago: Charles H. Kerr, 1912. A series of stories in the form of discussions between two children and their parents about the natural world. Gives explanations for why the social world is the way it is; also outlines elementary principles of biology.

Novikoff, Alex. *Climbing Our Family Tree.* New York: International Publishers, 1945. Explanation of evolution for children. This book does not use biological evolution as a metaphor for social evolution, as did the books of the Socialists, but it does take up social issues such as racism, albeit in a liberal, non-Marxist way. Novikoff, a biologist, was fired from the University of Vermont during the 1950s.

————. *From Head to Foot: Our Bodies and How They Work.* New York: International Publishers, 1946. Elementary human biology for children. Nothing in this book shows it to have been written and published by radicals.

Potamkin, Harry Alan, and Gertrude Rady. *Pioneer Song Book.* New York: New Pioneer Publishing, 1935. A collection of songs written for the Young Pioneers of America for use in Pioneer summer camps and troop meetings.

Red Corner Book for Children, The. New York: International Publishers, ca. 1932. A collection of stories and activities much like Beauchamp's *Martin's Annual* (1935—see listing above). First published in England in 1931, it contains a variety of stories—for example about miners' children in Appalachia, a letter from an American political prisoner in California to his daughter, stories about life in the Soviet Union, and "Why," from *Fairy Tales for Workers' Children.*

Riedman, Sarah R. *How Man Discovered His Body.* New York: International Publishers, 1947. A history of discoveries in human biology. Part of the Young World Series.

Segal, Edith, et al. *Victory Verses for Young Americans.* New York: International Workers Order, ca. 1942. A collection of poems by Segal on themes of anti-Fascism, with other poems, compiled by Segal, written by children. In the mid-1950s, Segal began to publish more books of poems, for both children and adults.

Selsam, Millicent E. *Egg to Chick.* New York: International Publishers, 1946. For very young children. Part of Young World Series.

————. *Hidden Animals.* New York: International Publishers, 1947. Another for very young children, about camouflage in the animal world. In the Young World Series.

Trease, Geoffrey. *Bows against the Barons.* New York: International Publishers, 1934. A radical re-telling of the story of Robin Hood for older children and adolescents.

———. *Comrades for the Charter.* New York: International Publishers, 1934. Two boys are brought into the charter agitation in Wales during the 1830s. Issues discussed include Welsh-English antagonism and the destruction of the Welsh countryside by the beginning of coal mining.

———. *Call to Arms.* New York: International Publishers, 1935. Three young people in a Central American country are drawn into a revolution when international arms merchants provoke a war. The setting seems to have been inspired by Nicaragua, in part, because of the giant lake near the capital city.

Wedding, Alex [Greta Weiskopf]. *Eddie and the Gypsy.* Trans. Charles Ashleigh. New York: International Publishers, 1935. A German working-class boy in Berlin during the 1930s confronts the hardships of his father's unemployment with the help of the son of Communists and a Gypsy girl. The author later, after going into exile from Germany, wrote *Das Eismeer ruft* (The ice ocean calls). London: Malik-Verlag, 1936.

Whitman, Walt. *I Hear the People Singing: Selected Poems of Walt Whitman.* Intro. Langston Hughes. New York: International Publishers, 1946. The title says it all.

The following three entries are related to the above although they do not fit into a listing of English-language, U.S.-published books. The first two came out of the English socialist movement and were never published in the United States. The third, in Finnish, was published for the Finnish Socialist Federation.

The Child's Socialist Reader. Illustrated by Walter Crane. London: Twentieth Century Press, 1907. A collection of stories by various authors presenting the kind of socialism advocated by William Morris. It includes short biographies of Karl Marx and William Morris, explanations of socialism, and parables teaching the morality of socialism.

Hazell, A. P. *The Red Catechism.* London: Twentieth Century Press, 1907. A series of lessons in the question-and-answer form of a religious catechism on "Socialist and Other Schools," "Socialism and the Working Class," "Landlordism," "Newspaper Boys," and other topics. It includes the socialist Ten Commandments, which were also included in *The Child's Socialist Reader* (see above).

Makela, A. B. *Aakosia Sosiallstien Lapsille* (Children's socialist alphabet). Fitchberg, MA: Finnish Socialist Federation, ca. 1912. The book's purpose was to teach Finnish as well as socialism to children.

conclusion

Between 1946 and 1956, the Communist Party endured a three-pronged crisis. By the late 1950s, much of the membership, including some who had led the party during its strongest periods, had left or, like Earl Browder, had been expelled. Party members were driven from influential positions in the CIO; the wide network of friends and allies that the CP had developed during the New Deal and the war years unraveled; and many party leaders were jailed under the terms of the Smith Act. The institutions that had formed the bedrock of the Communist political culture had disbanded or had been suppressed.

Then, in 1956, Krushchev's speech to the Twentieth Congress of the Communist Party of the Soviet Union (CPSU) detailing the extent of terror that had existed under Stalin—and moreover the Soviet suppression of the revolt in Hungary—sent shock waves through the Communist movement.[1] These events called into question a basic part of the ideology to that Communists had given much of their lives. After 1956, the Communist Party would not regain the influence it had during the 1930s and 1940s. The Communist Party itself was greatly reduced in membership, and the auxiliary organizations were in disarray.

The perception on the part of most Americans of a postwar bifurcation of the world between the United States and the Soviet Union—the beginning of the cold war—put Communists as well as non-Communist radicals on the defensive. As the international cold war expanded into a domestic "Red scare," the institutions in which the

Communist political culture had developed became more politically isolated, lost crucial sources of political and financial support, or were suppressed.

In 1950, the insurance examiner of the State of New York declared that the International Workers Order was a "Communist-allied" organization and revoked its charter to provide insurance. When the Supreme Court refused to hear the IWO's appeal, the order disbanded. What was left after its dissolution were small, independent fraternal societies and cultural groups, often organized around a foreign-language newspaper and serving an aging population.[2] The Jewish People's Fraternal Order of the IWO was the strongest and continues today as the Jewish Cultural Clubs and Societies. Its women's club continues as the Emma Lazarus Women's Clubs. Other Jewish cultural activities once sponsored by the IWO, such as the Freiheit choruses and the publication of Yiddish literature, continued at a much reduced level.[3]

In 1955, the Joint Legislative Committee on Charitable and Philanthropic Agencies and Organizations of the State of New York began an investigation of "possible subversive training and indoctrination of children in Communist-established summer camps."[4] The committee traced the history of Communist summer camps back to the 1920s, using the 1930 report of the U.S. Congressional Investigating Committee on Communist Propaganda to prove that the Communist Party had a "deliberate program to recruit children into the Communist Conspiracy."[5] There was no mention in the report of the fact that most of the children at these camps came from families that shared the ideals of the camps' organizers. During the committee hearings, all of the subpoenaed staff took the Fifth Amendment and refused to testify. Deciding not to ask children to testify, in part out of the recognition that this would be asking children to testify against their parents, the committee was able to find only one friendly witness. This was a young soldier, Stanley Wechkin, who had attended Kinderland for the two summers of 1947 and 1948.[6] Although no legal effort was made to close the cited camps in the aftermath of the investigation, Wo-Chi-Ca was closed following harassment from its neighbors and Kinderland was forced to move from the site it had occupied since 1923. The FBI threatened Camp Wynadot, which had absorbed Camp Wo-Chi-Ca, that the camp would be under constant surveillance if the two children of fugitive Communist leader Gil Green were allowed to attend. Fearful that the FBI presence would incite violence against the camp from the surrounding community, the camp management complied. The children were denied access.[7]

The repressive atmosphere of the times affected children from radical families at home as well in the left-wing institutions. In *Vengeance on the Young: The Story of the Smith Act Children,* left-wing author Albert Kahn detailed the harassment by the FBI and other government agencies of children of Communist leaders. This included having agents follow children to school, photographing them playing, and notifying teachers about their parents' "subversive activities."[8]

In June 1952, in response to the conviction of leading Communists under the Smith Act and the decision by the CP to send individual leaders "underground," Peggy Dennis and other wives of jailed Communist leaders formed the Families Committee of Smith Act Victims. Among its projected activities was the provision of support for the children of Communist leaders. The committee defined a program to deal with the psychological as well as material difficulties children of Communists faced in the midst of the "Red scare." Defining its goals, the committee stated:

> In planning the special program concerning the welfare and security of our children, we do so with this purpose in mind:
> a. To demonstrate in practical and tangible forms, and at times on levels understandable to children, that they are not alone because of their parents political beliefs.
> b. That they are loved, accepted and respected because they are children of Smith Act victims.
> c. That their needs and problems are the concern (or will be made the concern) of the labor and progressive movement, and that together, all these forces will fight for their fathers' and mothers' return.[9]

The Families Committee of Smith Act Victims would be the last organization Communists would create to deal with children, and because of the circumstances, its activities were primarily defensive.

The economic situation following the Second World War also changed the relationship between the Communist and American cultures. The prosperity of the war years and the postwar period gave increased security to the industrial labor force, although it did not come without fierce conflict and at a high cost.

Prosperity also meant new openings in white-collar occupations and the professions. Communists who had previously been economically as well as culturally and politically marginal began to get a taste of economic stability. In New York, particularly, free higher education gave children from radical working-class families entry into the middle class. For some, their very experiences in the radical movements of the 1930s and 1940s gave them skills that eased the process of upward mobility. Participants in the Communist movement developed organizational skills and a high level of literacy that were important in many white-collar occupations.

During this same period, many of the older working-class and ethnic communities were changing due to the postwar migration from the cities to the suburbs. As these communities changed, so did the radical movements that had been based there. Jerry Trauber, IWO junior director during the 1930s, reflected that one of the reasons that IWO children's activities declined after the Second World War was that many radicals, particularly Jewish radicals, participated in this exodus, which was accompanied by a shift from community orientation to a focus on the nuclear family.[10] Indeed, as historian Elaine Tyler May has pointed out, the pronounced 1950s emphasis on the nuclear family had more than a coincidental connection to the cold war and so-called Red scare. May argues that the scare focused on an internal weakness, feeding on Americans' postwar uneasiness with the successes of New Deal liberalism.[11] This led to the glorification of the nuclear family as the bulwark against subversion, both foreign and "domestic."

Although American Communists resisted the political tide, they too claimed loyalty to the new "domestic ideal."[12] Ironically, the crises in the institutions of the Communist Left led to the transformation of the Communist political culture from a public, political one to a culture centered in families and networks of families. That was where Communists defended themselves from repression and attempted to pass on their values to their children—at home.

The Communist political culture was not to vanish, even in the face of the threefold crisis in Communist politics. Previously I have emphasized the concerns of the adults who organized activities for children in the Communist political world; now, as those activities came to an end, we can get a glimpse of the continuities of that culture by looking at the children themselves, as they emerge politically from the 1950s.

Children of Communists from the 1930s and 1940s would, it turned out, play an important role in the New Left of the 1960s. For some of these children, exposure to the politics and worldview of the radical movement had come through organized children's activities such as summer camps and after-school programs. For others, particularly during the 1950s after the Scare and the internal crises of the Communist movement, radical politics was centered in the family and the informal networks of relatives and friends.

What these Red Diaper Babies, as they came to be called, brought to the New Left included the words to songs of the labor movement and the Spanish Civil War, a knowledge of the history of the American radical movement, and an often critical stance toward the United States' role in world affairs. More importantly, they were familiar with negotiating between the mainstream culture of America, which they considered to be conservative, jingoist, and conformist, and a culture of their own; one in which they built upon their parents' vision of an egalitarian, peaceful, and just society.

This was particularly true for girls, raised in Communist families during the 1950s, who were taught, both explicitly and often by example, a value system in which girls were expected to grow up as active and as publicly involved as their brothers. The importance of these Red Diaper Daughters for the emergence of the women's liberation movement of the late 1960s highlights the continuities between the Communist political culture of the 1930s and 1940s and the New Left of the 1960s.[13]

Many other roads led to the movements of the 1960s, of course. The social-democratic League for Industrial Democracy was the initial sponsor of Students for a Democratic Society (SDS), and organizations in the pacifist tradition such as the War Resisters League and the Fellowship of Reconciliation were more in evidence in terms of direct inspiration and involvement than was the Communist Party.[14] By the end of the decade, the New Left included many activists from apolitical or conservative family backgrounds.

Yet the children of Communists and former Communists played a special role in the New Left. It was noted early in the decade by the adversaries of the student protesters. In 1964, an article in *Young Guard,* the magazine of the conservative Young Americans for Freedom, disputed the "newness" of the then emerging New Left in Berkeley,

California. The article listed the names of forty-six young activists whose parents had been or continued to be members of the Communist Party. The article analyzed the causes of the Berkeley Free Speech Movement in terms of the family backgrounds of the student protesters: "For these 'second-generation' radicals the normal parent-child conflict is not taking place. . . . The fanaticism and articulateness of the red diaper babies is easily understood when one remembers that these youthful radicals are merely reiterating for the millionth time parental doctrines learned from the cradle."[15]

Often, second-generation radicals' influence on the New Left was felt through their personal relationships with activists from nonradical families who were finding their way to the movement. For example, Stokely Carmichael, prior to becoming a leader in the Student Non-Violent Coordinating Committee (SNCC) in the Southern civil rights movement, had been a high school friend of Eugene Dennis Jr., the son of the general secretary of the Communist Party during the 1950s.[16] Phil Ochs, the most strongly political of the new folksingers of the 1960s, had learned both his guitar playing and his radical politics from his college roommate Jim Glover, whose parents were radicals.[17] Although these relationships may not have been the central influence on their politics—the emerging civil rights movement and New Left drew in many with no contact with the "old" Left or its children—contact with so-called Red Diaper Babies may have made them more open to the new social movements.

Historical accounts of the movements of the 1960s have explored the issue of the radical family backgrounds of these New Left activists, at the same time emphasizing the differences between the ideology of the New Left and that of the Communist movement of the 1930s and 1940s. Kirkpatrick Sale, in his history of SDS, wrote:

> Probably only a handful of the early SDSers were true "red-diaper babies" . . . but since more than two million people went through the ranks of the Communist Party at one time or another in the thirties, and since there were millions more who moved in or near the other eddies of the left, it would not be surprising if a number of SDSers had some brush with the ideas of the left during their upbringing.[18]

James P. O'Brien estimated that more than one-third of politically active students during the 1960s were second-generation radicals. He commented that "generally these students . . . did not bring to college with them a well-formulated Marxist ideology. What they brought was a set of attitudes favorable to peace, civil liberties, and racial tolerance, as well as a willingness to act in support of these goals."[19]

The political culture of the Communist movement in the United States developed alongside the rise and decline of the Communist Party between 1923 and 1950. During this period, American Communists struggled to confront their own relationship with American culture in light of their experiences as immigrants, radicals, and workers, and in doing so they tried to bequeath an ideological and cultural legacy to their children. This political culture often defined the ways in which Communists dealt with their own political involvements and the daily life-experiences of working, raising a family, and acculturating themselves to American society. Although this culture was directly tied to the political perspectives of the Communist Party, it also maintained some degree of autonomy, for the issues in the culture were not always of central importance for the party. In some cases, as I have shown, the needs of the culture would come into conflict with the needs of the party. The transformation of this culture by Red Diaper Babies during the 1960s had its roots in the cultural changes that occurred in the Communist political culture during the 1920s, 1930s, and 1940s.

In the political culture of the American Communist movement, the vision of socialism as a world renewed and redefined evolved in the context of an ongoing revolutionary political movement. For the creators of that culture, socialism was destined to remain an ideal. Yet, if socialism in the United States has been more a dream than a practical possibility, I hope I have shown why it is important to understand the nature of the dream, not simply its lack of realization. Visions, unlike strategies, cannot fail. They can only be forgotten. This study has been an attempt to remember the dream so that it may enrich our current political reality—dismal as it may seem now.

notes

Chapter 1. Introduction

1. Calvin Trillin, "U.S. Journal: The Bronx," *New Yorker* (1 August 1977), p. 50.

2. See David Kertzer, *Comrades and Christians: Religion and Political Struggle in Communist Italy* (Cambridge: Cambridge University Press, 1980), passim, for an analysis of the separation between family and politics in the Communist movement in northern Italy.

3. For the view that Soviet influence was the primary historical issue in the history of the Communist Party in the United States, see Theodore Draper, *The Roots of American Communism* (New York: Viking Press, 1957) and *American Communism and Soviet Russia* (New York: Viking Press, 1960); and Harvey Klehr, *The Heyday of American Communism: The Depression Decade* (New York: Basic Books, 1984). For research contesting this view and that has seen the CP as an expression of American radicalism, see Maurice Isserman, *Which Side Were You On? The American Communist Party during the Second World War* (Middletown, CT: Weslyan University Press, 1982); Mark Naison, *Communists in Harlem during the Great Depression* (Champaign: University of Illinois Press, 1983); Robin Kelley, *Hammer and Hoe: Alabama Communists during the Great Depression* (Chapel Hill: University of North Carolina Press, 1990); and the collection of essays by Michael Brown et al., *New Studies in the Politics and Culture of U.S. Communism* (New York: Monthly Review Press, 1993). Draper has responded to his critics in two lengthy essays, "The Popular Front Revisited," *New York Review of Books*, 30 May 1985, and "American Communism Revisited," *New York Review of Books*, 9 May 1985.

4. Friedrich Engels, "The Labor Movement in the United States" (1887), in Lewis S. Feuer, ed., *Marx and Engels: Basic Writings in Politics and Philosophy* (Garden City, NY: Doubleday, 1959), p. 494.

5. For Gastonia, see Liston Pope, *Millhands and Preachers: A Study of Gastonia*

(New Haven: Yale University Press, 1942), and Theodore Draper, "Gastonia Revisited" *Social Research* 38 (spring 1971). For the National Miners Union, see Linda Nyden, "Black Miners in Western Pennsylvania, 1925–1931: The NMU and the UMW," *Science and Society* 41 (spring 1977): 69–101.

6. Serge Denisoff, *Songs of Protest, War and Peace: A Bibliography and Discography* (Santa Barbara, CA: ABC-Clio, 1973), pp. 22, 23.

7. Pete Seeger, *The Incompleat Folksinger* (New York: Simon & Schuster, 1972), p. 72.

8. Archie Green, *Only a Miner* (Urbana: University of Illinois Press, 1972), pp. 78, 79.

9. Ibid., p. 420.

10. See Robbie Lieberman, *"My Song Is My Weapon": People's Songs, American Communism, and the Politics of Culture, 1930–1956* (Urbana: University of Illinois Press, 1989); Robert Cantweel, *When We Were Young: The Folk Song Revival* (Cambridge, MA: Harvard University Press, 1996); and Ronald Cohen and Dave Samuelson, *Songs for Political Action: Folk Music, Topical Songs and the American Left* (Hambergen, Germany: Bear Family Records, 1996), passim.

11. Friedrich Engels, *Socialism: Utopian and Scientific* (New York: International, 1935), pp. 72–73.

12. Eric Hobsbawm, *Primitive Rebels* (New York: W. W. Norton, 1959), p. 57.

13. Michelle Weinroth, *Reclaiming William Morris: Englishness, Sublimity and the Rhetoric of Dissent* (Montreal: McGill–Queen's University Press, 1996), p. 13.

14. For a discussion of these and similar efforts by American Marxian socialists, see the following: for Llano del Rio and Newllano, Robert Hine, *California Utopian Communities* (Berkeley: University of California Press, 1983); for Ruskin, Tennessee, John Egerton, "Visions of Utopia," *Southern Exposure* (March 1979): 38–47; for Ruskin, Florida, Lori Robinson and Bill De Yong, "Socialism in the Sunshine: The Roots of Ruskin, Florida," *Tampa Bay History* (spring/summer 1982).

15. William Cobb, "From Utopian Isolation to Radical Activism: Commonwealth College, 1925–1935," *Arkansas Historical Quarterly* 32 (summer 1973): 132.

16. Mike Gold, "A Little Bit of Millennium," in Michael Folsom, ed. *Mike Gold: A Literary Anthology* (New York: International, 1972), p. 72.

17. Betsy Blackmar, "Going to the Mountains: A Social History," in *Resorts of the Catskills* (New York: St. Martin's Press, 1979), p. 86.

18. Daniel Bell, *The Tamiment Library,* Bibliographical Series no.6 (New York: New York University Libraries, 1969), p. 24.

19. Sophie Saroff and Arthur Tobier, *Stealing the State, Sophie Saroff: An Oral History* (New York: Community Documentation Workshop, 1983), pp. 20, 21.

20. Paul Avrich, *An American Anarchist: The Life of Voltairine De Cleyre* (Princeton: Princeton University Press, 1978), p. 115*n*; Maximilian Hurwitz, *The*

Workmen's Circle: Its History, Ideals, Organization, and Institutions (New York: The Workmen's Circle, 1936), p.191.

21. Jenna Weissman Joselit with Karen S. Mittelman, eds., *A Worthy Use of Summer: Jewish Summer Camping in America* (Philadelphia: National Museum of American Jewish History, 1993), passim.

22. Much has been made of the decision of the Sixth Congress of the Communist International to propose an independent black republic in the American South. More important for the thinking of American Communists on race were other resolutions—one on the importance of fighting for full social and political equality for African Americans and another on fighting "white chauvinism" within the ranks of the CP: Naison, *Communists in Harlem,* p. 4. The Communist Party became the first, and at that time the only, predominantly white organization to treat the concerns of African Americans as of paramount importance.

23. Naison, *Communists in Harlem;* Nell Irvin Painter, *The Narrative of Hosea Hudson* (Cambridge, MA: Harvard University Press, 1979); and Kelley, *Hammer and Hoe.*

24. See Wilson Record, *The Negro and the Communist Party* (Chapel Hill: University of North Carolina Press, 1951) and Harold Cruse, *The Crisis of the Negro Intellectual* (New York: Morrow, 1967).

25. Rosalyn Baxandall, "The Question Seldom Asked: Women and the CPUSA," in Brown et al., *New Studies,* p. 161n.

26. Both these positions were often held by American Socialists and the IWWs out of which the Communist Party was created.

27. Van Gosse, "To Organize in Every Neighborhood, in Every Home: The Gender Politics of American Communists between the Wars," *Radical History Review* 50 (spring 1991): 133.

Chapter 2. The Littlest Proletariat

1. Sidney Ditzion, *Marriage, Morals, and Sex in America: A History of Ideas* (New York: Bookman Associates, 1953), p. 281.

2. Karl Marx and Frederick Engels, *Manifesto of the Communist Party* (New York: International, 1975), p. 27.

3. Arthur W. Calhoun, *A Social History of the American Family from Colonial Times to the Present,* 4 vols. (Cleveland, OH: Arthur Clark, 1919), 3:326.

4. Frederick Engels, *The Origins of the Family, Private Property and the State* (New York: International, 1963), p. 65.

5. Lewis Coser, introduction to *Women under Socialism,* by August Bebel (New York: Schocken, 1971), p. vii.

6. Ditzion, *Marriage, Morals and Sex,* p. 292.

7. Bebel, *Woman under Socialism,* p. 349.

8. Ibid., p. 344.

9. Vernon Lidtke, *Alternative Culture: Socialist Labor in Imperial Germany* (New York: Oxford University Press, 1985), p. 186.

10. Coser, introduction to *Women under Socialism.*

11. John Spargo, *Applied Socialism* (New York: B. W. Huebsch, 1912), p. 243.

12. David Goldstein, *Socialism: A Nation of Fatherless Children,* Martha Moore Avery, ed. (Boston: Union News League, 1903), p. 228.

13. Morris Hillquit and Father John Ryan, *Socialism: Promise or Menace?* (New York: Macmillan, 1914), p. 151.

14. John Spargo, *Socialism and Motherhood* (New York: B. W. Huebsch, 1914), p. 30.

15. Ibid., p. 53.

16. See Ruth Bordin, *Women and Temperance: The Quest for Power and Liberty, 1873–1900* (Philadelphia: Temple University Press, 1981). Bordin argues that the WCTU can be seen as a protofeminist organization fighting in defense of feminine values against the combined masculinist forces of politics and the marketplace.

17. Quoted in Mari Jo Buhle, *Women and American Socialism, 1870–1920* (Urbana: University of Illinois Press, 1981), p. 65.

18. *The Child of the Worker: A Collection of Facts and the Remedy* (Berlin-Schweneberg: Publishing House of the Young Communist International, 1923), p. 45.

19. Questions about the 1920s' oft-noted prosperity have been raised by historian Frank Stricker. Stricker's comments support the Communist view of working-class misery in that decade: he writes that

> the outpouring of goods and the creation of needs in the 1920s supports the decade's reputation as the first excursion into mass affluence. But the masses were not affluent enough to worry much about clean-smelling breath and fancy cars. Wages were higher than in the pre-war period, but for many increased little after 1923. Unemployment did not disappear and the annual earnings of many workers were inadequate to support basic needs. Perhaps 40 percent of the population was poor in the 1920s. So many unskilled workers had to use social agencies and free services that contemporaries found it hard to delineate a poverty line separating independent families from dependent ones.
>
> "Affluence for Whom? Another Look at Prosperity and the Working Classes in the 1920s," in Daniel J. Leab, *The Labor History Reader* (Urbana: University of Illinois Press, 1985), p. 315.

20. Grace Hutchins. *Children under Capitalism*, International Pamphlets no. 33 (New York: Labor Research Associates, 1932), p. 3.

21. Ibid., p. 17.

22. James Mickel Williams, *Human Aspects of Unemployment and Relief* (Chapel

Hill: University of North Carolina Press, 1933), pp. 54, 55.

23. Hutchins, *Children under Capitalism,* p. 8.

24. Cited in Labor Research Association, *Labor Fact Book 5* (New York: International, 1941), p. 68.

25. Adelaide Walker, "Child Slavery in Colorado Beet Fields," *Workers Life* (July/August 1932): 6.

26. David I. MacLeod, *Building Character in the American Boy: The Boy Scouts, YMCA, and Their Forerunners, 1870–1920* (Madison: University of Wisconsin Press, 1983), p. 4.

27. Ibid., pp. 15–16.

28. David Nasaw, *Children of the City at Work and at Play* (Garden City, NY: Anchor Press/Doubleday, 1985), p. 24.

29. Both MacLeod and Nasaw show how reformers' efforts to save working-class children from the dangers of the streets, both real and imagined, were characterized by strong efforts at social control. Working-class children, especially boys, were seen as problems both because they had less parental control and because their lives did not conform to middle-class expectations. See Nasaw, *Children of the City,* chapters 2 and 10, passim, and MacLeod, *Building Character,* chapter 2, passim.

30. Nasaw, *Children of the City,* p. 140.

31. *Child of the Worker,* p. 20.

32. Ibid., p. 21.

33. Edwin Hoernle, *A Manual for Leaders of Children's Groups* (Berlin: Young Communist International, n.d.), p. 17. Hoernle wrote a larger work on this subject, published only in German: *Grundfragen der Proletarischen Erziehung* (Basic questions of Communist education) (Berlin: Verlag der Jugendinternationale, 1929). I am grateful to Leonard Herman for translating Walter Benjamin's review of this book.

34. *Child of the Worker*, p. 54.

35. U.S. Congress. House. Special Committee to Investigate Communist Activities, *Investigation of Communist Propaganda,* 71st Cong., 2nd sess. (Washington, DC: 1930), part 3, vol. 1, p. 66; and Ernest Rymer, personal interview, January 1982.

36. Sam Darcy Papers. Folder: Young Pioneers/Young Worker's League, Tamiment Library, New York City.

37. *Child of the Worker,* p. 17.

38. Jocelyn Tien, "Educational Theories of American Socialists, 1900–1920." Ph.D. diss., Michigan State University, 1973, p. 111.

39. Kenneth Teitelbaum, *Schooling For "Good Rebels": Socialist Education for Children in the United States, 1900–1920* (Philadelphia: Temple University Press, 1993), p. 38.

40. *New York Tribune,* 14 April 1919. Clipping in the papers of the Lusk

Committee, New York State Library, Albany, NY, box 4, file 11.

41. *Progressive Journal of Education* (Chicago, 1909–1910), passim.

42. MS from information department of the Socialist Party National Office, n.d. Socialist Party Papers, reel 2070. Shedd put together a songbook for use in the Socialist Sunday schools that contained more than one hundred songs. Shedd was author of most of the lyrics. Kendrick Shedd, *Some Songs for Socialist Singers* (Rochester, NY: 1913).

43. David P. Berenberg, "Socialist Education," *Socialist World* (15 August 1920), quoted in K. Teitelbaum and W. Reese, "American Socialist Pedagogy and Experimentation in the Progressive Era: The Socialist Sunday School," *History of Education Quarterly* 23 (winter 1983): 436.

44. It would be a mistake to make too much of the differences between anarchists and Socialists during this period. Teitelbaum and Reese point out that a number of Socialist Sunday school teachers also taught at modern schools, and Socialist periodicals often reported the activities of the modern-school movement along with the activities of the Socialist Sunday schools. Teitelbaum and Reese, "American Socialist Pedagogy," p. 433. The *New York Times* (8 May 1910, p. 8) reported that anarchist Alexander Berkman attended that year's Workmen's Circle convention.

45. See Paul Avrich, *The Modern School Movement: Anarchism and Education in the United States* (Princeton: Princeton University Press, 1980), passim, for a full discussion of these anarchist efforts.

46. B. Liber, *The Child and the Home: Essays in the Rational Bringing-up of Children* (New York: Vanguard Press, 1927), p. 58.

47. Avvo Kostiainen, *The Forging of Finnish-American Communism: A Study in Ethnic Radicalism* (Turko, Finland: Turun Yliopisto, 1978), p. 175.

48. In his essay "Bolshevism and the Anarchists," E. J. Hobsbawm discussed the relationship between Communists and anarchists during the 1920s. He pointed out that despite the history of antagonism between Marxists and anarchists dating back to Marx, Communist parties in their early years saw anarchism as a politically healthy response to reformist socialism, and in some countries (France, Brazil, and Cuba, among others) much of the membership of the new CPs was made up of workers who had been members of anarchist and anarcho-syndicalist trade unions. He does not take up the case of the United States, but this mutual sympathy did exist here. E. J. Hobsbawm, *Revolutionaries* (New York: New American Library, 1973), p. 57.

49. Avrich, *Modern School Movement,* p. 253.

50. William Thurston Brown, "Citizenship and Education," MS (Stelton, N.J.: Ferrer Colony, n.d. but approx. 1920), p. 28.

51. Eden and Cedar Paul, *Proletcult* (New York: Thomas Seltzer, 1921), p. 70.

52. Hugo Gellert, "Teachers Who Flunk," *The New Masses* (March 1930): 13.

53. *The Worker's Child* 1 (January 1934): 1.

54. Hoernle, *Manual for Leaders,* p. 53.

55. Young Workers (Communist) League of America, *Bulletin on the*

Reorganization of Pioneer Groups, November 1925, MS in the Sam Darcy Collection. Folder: Young Workers League/Young Pioneers, Tamiment Library, New York University.

56. Hoernle, *Manual for Leaders,* p. 6.

57. Ibid., p. 19.

58. See John Bodnar, *The Transplanted* (Bloomington: Indiana University Press, passim, for a discussion of the multiple ways that immigrants during this period constructed ethnic cultural institutions to comfort themselves and to transmit their cultures to their children.

59. Mary Kingsbury, *Socialism as an Educative and Social Force on the East Side* (Boston: Publications of the Christian Social Union, 1898), p. 11.

60. Liber, *The Child and the Home,* p. 80.

61. Teitelbaum and Reese, "American Socialist Pedagogy," p. 432.

62. Arthur Liebman, *Jews and the Left* (New York: John Wiley, 1979), p. 212.

63. S. Yefroiken, "Yiddish Secular Schools in the United States," in Salo Baron et al., eds ., *Jewish People Past and Present,* vol. 2 (New York: Jewish Encyclopedic Handbooks, Central Yiddish Culture Organization, 1948), p. 144.

64. Maximillian Hurwitz, *The Workmen's Circle: Its History, Ideals, Organization, and Institutions* (New York: Workmen's Circle, 1936), pp. 167–68.

65. Liebman, *Jews and the Left,* p. 298.

66. The Hall Socialism of the Finns represented one of the strongest alternative cultures within the American Socialist movement. The Finns were often criticized by other Socialists, and later Communists, for neglecting the class struggle in favor of building the culture of their own communities.

67. John I. Kolehmainen, *The Finns in America: A Bibliographical Guide to Their History* (Hancock, Michigan: Finnish American Historical Library, Suomi College, 1947), pp. 92, 104.

68. Sophie Gerson, personal interview, February 1984.

69. Ernest Rymer, personal interview, January 1982.

70. Max Bedacht, *The Organizer and His Problems: A Manual for Builders of the I.W.O.* (New York: International Workers Order, n.d.—ca. 1935), p. 9.

71. Jerry Trauber, "For the Juniors," *New Order* 7 (May/June 1938): 22.

Chapter 3. The Young Pioneers of America and the Communist Children's Movement: 1922–1934

1. Elizabeth Sharnoff, "Organize Future Socialists," *Falconry: A Fortnightly for Falcon Guides* (Chicago: Red Falcons of America), no. 6 (30 June 1936): 2; in Socialist Party Papers, microfilm reel 2074, Tamiment Library.

2. In those areas where the Communist Party was a significant political force (for example, among radical ethnic groups) children from non-Communist families might become Pioneers. In working-class communities where there were no other organized children's activities, the Young Pioneers could recruit off the street.

3. Young Workers (Communist) League of America, *Bulletin on the Reorganization of Pioneer Groups* (November 1925), MS in the Sam Darcy Collection, folder on Young Workers League/Young Pioneers, Tamiment Library, New York University.

4. R. M. Whitney, *Reds in America* (New York: Beckwith Press, 1924), p. 98.

5. Ibid., p. 99.

6. *New Pioneer* 4, no. 5 (September 1935): 21.

7. Martha Campion, *Who Are the Young Pioneers?*, illustrated by Mary Morrow (New York: New Pioneer Publishing, 1934), back cover.

8. *New Pioneer* 3, no. 6 (October 1934): 1.

9. "Some Experiences in Troop Leadership—Good and Bad," *Worker's Child* 1 (January 1934): 8.

10. The Pioneers' campaign against the Boy Scouts was based on a long-standing radical critique of Scouting as a pro-imperialist, militarist movement. Before the First World War, Socialist Party women denounced the Boy Scouts as an effort "on the part of capitalists and military men to control the education of children in their youth and develop a military-minded race, trained to 'unquestioning obedience,' to do the will of the masters and uphold the tottering domination of the capitalist class." Mary O'Reilly, *The Boy Scout Movement* (Chicago: Women's National Committee of the Socialist Party, n.d.), Tamiment Library pamphlet files, #6247.

11. U.S. Congress. House. *Hearings before a Special Committee to Investigate Communist Activities in the United States.* (Washington, D.C.: 1930) (hereafter, U.S. House. Fish Committee), part 3, vol. 1, p. 23.

12. Ibid., p. 39.

13. Preva Glusman and Morris Colman, "WIR Children's Center–New York," *Workers Life* (organ of the WIR) (June 1932): 20.

14. Ibid.: 21.

15. *New Pioneer* 2 (October 1932): 5.

16. *Young Pioneer* 5 (June/July 1928): 2.

17. Eda Beck (Harry Eisman's sister), personal interview, 16 September 1984. Harry returned to the United States for visits several times. In the Soviet Union he remained a committed Communist until he died on 8 May 1979. On 19 May 1984, his sisters placed a memorial notice in the *Daily World*, noting that a monument on his grave in Moscow, erected by the Pioneers of the Soviet Union, was inscribed: "Harry Eisman, Americansky Pioneer" (clipping from collection of Eda Beck, n.d.). Eda married and in the 1930s left New York for California, where she and her husband became quite wealthy in real-estate investment. Eda continued to support the Communist Party, both politically and financially.

18. Harry Eisman, *An American Boy in the Soviet Union* (New York: Youth Publishers, 1934), p. 5.

19. U.S. House. Fish Committee, 1930, part 3, vol. 1, p. 19.

20. Eisman's political views at the end of his life can be found in the transcrip-

tion of a discussion between him and his sister Eda Beck that took place in Los Angeles in the mid-1970s. A typescript copy of the transcript MS is in the author's possession.

21. Harvey Klehr, *Communist Cadre* (Stanford, CA: Hoover Institution Press, 1978), p.24.

22. Martha Campion, *Who Are the Young Pioneers?* (New York: New Pioneer, 1934), passim.

23. Sophie Gerson, personal interview, 12 February 1984.

24. Ernest Rymer, personal interview, January 1982.

25. *New Pioneer* 7 (November 1932): 22.

26. U.S. House. Fish Committee, part 9, vol. 1, pp. 1 and 13.

27. *Työmies* (Superior, WI), 6 November 1932, p. 4.

28. *Työmies*, 18 May 1932, p. 3.

29. Ethel Kirschner, personal interview with the author, November 1986, at Camp Midvale, New Jersey, which had been a Nature Friends Camp until it was burned down by the Ku Klux Klan in the 1950s.

30. *New Pioneer* 1 (New York) (1 July 1931): 12.

31. *By-Laws of the Slovak Worker's Society* (New Jersey: Slovak Worker's Society, 1926), p.45.

32. *New Pioneer* 2 (August/September 1932): 18.

33. *New Pioneer* 3 (March 1934): 25.

34. *New Pioneer* 2 (May 1932): 9.

35. Mary Heaton Vorse, *The Passaic Textile Strike, 1926–1927* (Passaic, NJ: General Relief Committee of Textile Strikers, 1927), p. 40.

36. Ibid., pp. 41, 42.

37. Sophie Gerson, personal interview, 12 February 1984. See also Martha Stone Asher, "Recollections of the Passaic Textile Strike of 1926," *Labor's Heritage* (April 1990), p. 15.

38. Vorse, *Passaic*, pp. 91, 92.

39. *Young Comrade* 10 (June/July 1928): 8.

40. Daniel Georgianna and Roberta H. Aaronson, *The Strike of '28* (New Bedford, MA: Spinner, 1993), p. 85.

41. *New Pioneer* 1 (September 1931): 17.

42. Theodore Draper, "Gastonia Revisited," *Social Research* 38 (spring 1971),: 16.

43. Supreme Court of North Carolina, Fourteenth District, *State v. Fred Erwin Beal et al.,* spring 1930, no.456, pp. 252–257.

44. Ernest Rymer, personal interview, January 1982.

45. Rymer interview, January 1982.

46. Lauren Gilfillan (Harriet Woodbridge Gillfillan, *pseud.*), *I Went to Pit College* (New York: Literary Guild, 1934), p. 21.

47. "Dear Pioneers and Workers' Children," *New Pioneer* 1 (September 1931): 14.

48. For a further analysis of the discovery and use of protest folkmusic in the Communist political culture, see my discussion of Camp Woodland in chapter 6.

49. Gerald Zahavi, " 'Who's Going to Dance with Somebody Who Calls You a Mainstreeter?' Communism, Culture, and Community in Sheridan County, Montana, 1918–1934," *Great Plains Quarterly* 16 (fall 1996): 251–86. This article contains an extensive discussion of the Communist presence in Sheridan County.

50. The WPA guide to Montana says of Plentywood:

> The people here have been notably independent in politics. They began, mildly enough, by supporting the Bull Moose ticket in 1912. In 1918 the Non-Partisan League established the *Producers News* here, which under the editorship of Charles E. Taylor helped to build up an organization that on several occasions attracted national attention. From 1920 to 1926 nearly the entire population of Sheridan County belonged to the Farmer-Labor Party. . . .
>
> In 1930 about 500 citizens of the county voted the Communist Party ticket straight.

WPA Federal Writer's Project for Montana, *Montana: A State Guide Book* (New York: Viking, 1937), p. 225.

51. Zahavi, "Who's Going to Dance?" p. 268.

52. *Producers News,* Plentywood, Montana, 11 March 1932, p. 1.

53. Camp Kinderland, which began in 1925, was one of the few permanent camps set up during the 1920s. The association that operated the camp owned the land—a situation that prevailed more for camps operated during the 1930s and 1940s.

54. *People vs. Mintz*, 106 Cal. App. 725 290 Pac 93, (1930). Reporter's transcript, p. 297.

55. *Young Comrade* 5, no. 4: 6.

56. *Työmies*, 18 July 1930, p. 9.

57. Elizabeth Dilling, *The Red Network* (Kenilworth, IL: published by the author, 1934; reprint, New York: Arno, 1977), p. 249.

58. Rose Pastor Stokes, "Gastonia and Negro Children Given Vacation," *Solidarity: Official Organ of the Workers International Relief, American Section* 1, no.3 (August 1929): 2.

59. *Työmies*, 2 July 1930, p. 3.

60. *Työmies*, 29 May 1930, p. 5.

61. *People vs. Mintz*, reporter's transcript, p. 49.

62. *Työmies*, 9 July 1932, p. 3.

63. U.S. House. Fish Committee, part 5, vol. 3, p. 239.

64. Ibid.

65. *New Pioneer* 1 (August 1931): 18.

66. *People vs. Mintz*, reporter's transcript, p. 728.

67. See chapter 6 for a full discussion of children's literature published by the Communist Party during this period.

68. Harry Alan Potamkin and Gertrude Rady, *Pioneer Song Book*, 2nd edn. (New York: New Pioneer Publishing, 1935), pp. 8, 15. The first of these songs was cited in Gilfillan, *I Went*, p. 29.

69. Stokes, "Gastonia," p. 2.

70. Ibid.

71. *Työmies*, 10 July 1932, p. 3.

72. *Työmies*, 29 July 1930, p. 3.

73. *New Pioneer* 1 (New York, June 1931): 12.

Chapter 4. "Americans All! Immigrants All!"

1. For a variety of perspectives on this change see Georgi Dimitrov, *The United Front Against Fascism* (New York: New Century, 1945). Dimitrov was the Bulgarian Communist leader whose position at the Seventh Congress of the Communist International promoted Communist alliances with Socialists and liberals against Fascism. Earl Browder, *The People's Front* (New York: International Publishers, 1938). Browder led the U.S. Communist Party leadership regarding the change in line. Harvey Klehr, *The Heyday of American Communism: The Depression Decade* (New York: Basic Books, 1984) reflects a current anti-communist historical approach, while Michael Denning, *The Cultural Front* (New York: Verso, 1996) reflects a view more sympathetic with the Communists, especially in the cultural realm.

2. For a description of the beginnings of the IWO and the role of the IWO in the development of Communist perspectives on ethnicity in the United States see Roger Keeran, "National Groups and the Popular Front: The Case of the International Workers Order," *Journal of American Ethnic History* 14 (spring 1995): passim.

3. Judah J. Shapiro, *The Friendly Society, A History of the Workmen's Circle* (New York: Media Judaica, 1970), p. 84.

4. Ibid., p. 112.

5. Roger Keeran, "National Groups," pp. 26, 27.

6. Ibid., p. 33.

7. Auvo Kostianen, "For or Against Americanization?: The Case of the Finnish Immigrant Radicals," in Dirk Hoerder, ed., *American Labor and Immigration History: 1877–1920s: Recent European Research*, (Urbana, IL: University of Illinois Press, 1983), p. 263.

8. Paul Hummasti, *Finnish Radicals in Astoria, Oregon, 1904–1940* (New York: Arno Press, 1979), p. 298.

9. Ernest Rymer, personal interview, January 1982.

10. Max Bedacht, *Labor Fraternalism* (New York: National Education Department of the IWO, 1941), passim.

11. Steve Nelson, et al., *Steve Nelson, American Radical* (Pittsburgh, PA: University of Pittsburgh Press, 1981), p. 283.

12. *New Order* (New York) 7 (May/June 1938): 22.

13. Max Bedacht, *Labor Fraternalism*, p. 23.

14. Jerry Trauber, personal interview, September 15, 1982.

15. Jerry Trauber, "Report to the Fifth National Convention, Third National Junior Conference, IWO," mimeo, 1940, n.p., IWO Papers, Catherwood Library, Cornell University.

16. Jerry Trauber, "Children's Work in the IWO," in *The Worker's Child*, 1 (January 1934): 13.

17. Ibid.

18. Ibid.: 14.

19. Ibid.

20. Max Bedacht, "The Organizer and His Problems: A Manual for Builders of the IWO," n.d., MS, IWO Papers, Catherwood Library, Cornell University.

21. *New Order* (New York) 5 (April 1936): 19.

22. National Department for Children's Activities, *Building the Junior Lodge: A Handbook for Junior Directors* (New York: International Workers Order, 1946), p. 15, Jesus Colon Papers, subject file box 3, folder 1.

23. Martha Millet, *The Hungarian People: Their Traditions and Contributions* (New York: National Education Department, Junior Section–IWO, n.d.), p. 1.

24. Ibid., p. 5.

25. Ibid., p. 2.

26. National Department for Children's Activities, *Trips and Outings for Juniors* (New York: International Workers Order, n.d.), p. 7, Jesus Colon Papers, series 8, subject file box 3, file 1.

27. "Role of Youth in the Development of Our Fraternal Life," MS, n.a., n.d. (ca. late 1930s), Jesus Colon Papers, series 8, box 2.

28. Mark Naison, "Lefties and Righties: The Communist Party and Sports During the Great Depression," in Donald Spivey, ed., *Sports in America*, (Westport, CT: Greenwood Press, 1985), p. 138.

29. "Fraternalism and Worker's Children," *Five Years, IWO*, (New York: National Executive Committee of the IWO, 1935), p. 78.

30. *Report of the General Secretary, Brother Max Bedacht to the Fourth National Convention of the IWO*, (Pittsburgh, PA: IWO, 1938), p. 41.

31. Jerry Trauber, "Join the Parade," *New Order* 5 (September 1938): 4.

32. "Cleveland Has a Kid Camp," *New Order* 6 (June 1937): 20.

33. *Report of the Junior Section to the Fourth National Convention of the IWO*, mimeo, IWO Papers, Catherwood Library, Cornell University, p. 7.

34. *Proceedings of National Conference, Labor's Children in a World at War* (New York: Junior Section, IWO, 1941), p. 16.

35. Ibid., p. 21.

36. Roger Keeran, "National Groups": 45.

37. *Labor's Children in a World at War*, p. 1.

38. Jerry Trauber, personal interview, September 15, 1982.

39. National Department for Children's Activities, *Building the Junior Lodge*, p. 6.

40. *Report of the Junior Section*, p. 4.

41. *Report of the General Secretary, Brother Max Bedacht*, p. 64.

42. Jerry Trauber, personal interview, September 15, 1982.

43. "Report on the Work Done by the Cervantes Fraternal Society of the IWO from the Last Meeting of the General Council (September 1945–January 1946)," MS, Jesus Colon Papers, series 5, box 5, folder 8.

44. National Department for Children's Activities, *Building the Junior Lodge*, p. 6.

45. *IWO Schools Register*, IWO Papers, box 26, Catherwood Library, Cornell University.

46. *New Pioneer* (New York) 2 (May 1932): 28.

47. *New Pioneer* (New York) 1 (December 1931): 22.

48. *New Pioneer* (New York) 1 and 2 (1931–1932): passim. IWO *shules* would send greetings to the *New Pioneer* as a way of giving financial support to the magazine.

49. A. Meisel and Betzalel Friedman, *Workers School Textbook for the Third Year*, 1st ed. (New York: IWO, 1934), trans. Jacob Stachel, p. 6.

50. Ibid., p. 7.

51. Ibid., pp. 112, 113, and index.

52. Ibid., p. 100.

53. Ernest Rymer, personal interview, January 1982.

54. Itche Goldberg (director of the schools for the IWO), personal interview, September 1982.

55. Itche Goldberg, IWO Papers, Catherwood Library, Cornell University, n.d.

56. *Survey of Jewish Education in Los Angeles Carried Out by the Jewish Bureau of Education*, n.d. (ca.1945), p. 22, IWO Papers, Catherwood Library, Cornell University.

57. *Your Child* (New York: National Cultural and School Committee of the Jewish-American Section, IWO, 1943), p. 2.

Chapter 5. Socialism in One Summer

1. State of New York, Records of the Joint Legislative Committee on Charitable and Philanthropic Agencies and Organizations, 1956.

2. Maximilian Hurwitz, *The Workmen's Circle: Its History, Ideals, Organization and Institutions* (New York: Workmen's Circle, 1936), p. 191.

3. John Beck, "With the Children of the Working Class Lies the Future of America," unpublished paper on the Pioneer Youth of America.

4. John Beck, "Highlander's Junior Union Camps, 1940–1944: Workers' Children and Working Class Culture," *Labor's Heritage* 5 (spring 1993).

5. Leibush Lehrer, *The Objectives of Camp Boiberik: In Light of Its History* (New York: Camp Boiberik, 1962), p. 15.

6. *New Pioneer* 7 (August 1939): 19.

7. Arthur Tobier, *Stealing the State, Sophie Saroff: An Oral History* (New York: Community Documentation Workshop, l983), p. 32.

8. Ibid., p. 20. See references to the Coops in chapters 1 and 2.

9. State of New York police files, *Investigation of Communist Influence in Summer Camps*, 18 April 1947, p. 1. In New York State Library, Albany.

10. Tobier, *Stealing the State,* p. 21.

11. Elliott Arnold, "Comrades on Vacation," *New York World-Telegram*, 2–7 August 1937.

12. Ibid., 2 August, p. 17.

13. Ibid., 6 August, p. 15.

14. *New Order* 6 (June 1937): 20.

15. Jerry Trauber, national junior director, *Report to the Fifth National Convention, Third National Junior Conference, IWO,* June 1940, p. 12, and Jerry Trauber, personal interview, 15 September 1982.

16. FBI Files on Camp Kinderland, 13 July 1953, quoting Sol Vail, 16 November 1952. In New York State Library, Albany.

17. Daniel Bell, *Marxian Socialism in the United States* (Ithaca: Cornell University Press, 1967) (1952), p. 5.

18. *Kinderland, Book of the First Camp Kinderland Reunion* (New York: Camp Kinderland, 1979), p. 28.

19. Maximilian Hurwitz, *The Workmen's Circle: Its History, Ideals, Organization and Institutions* (New York: Workmen's Circle, 1936), p. 191.

20. *Kinderland*, p. 6.

21. Hurwitz, *Workmen's Circle,* p. 191.

22. *Kinderland*, p. 6.

23. Ibid., p. 2.

24. Writer Eugene Goodheart remembers reciting Feffer's Yiddish poem "Ich Bin a Yid," ("I am A Jew") while Feffer was visiting Kinderland during the 1930s. Eugene Goodheart, "I am A Jew," *Culturefront* 5, no. 3, and 6, no. 1 (winter 1997): 62.

25. Biographical information on Edith Segal is from Deborah Jowitt, "Edith Segal Dances into the Eighties," *Village Voice*, 6 July 1982, p. 75, and author's personal interview, November 1982.

26. Stacey Prickett, "Dance and the Workers' Struggle," *Dance Research* (London) 8 (spring 1990): 51.

27. Ibid.: 52.

28. Lawrence Emery, "Immigrants All! Americans All!" *Daily Worker* (New York), 31 July 1939, p. 2.

29. Ibid.

30. "Going Wo-Chi-Ca Way," *Wo-Chi-Ca Yearbook* (New Jersey: Camp Wo-Chi-Ca, 1949), n.p.

31. Ernest Rymer, personal interview, January 1982.

32. *Wo-Chi-Ca Yearbook.*

33. Milton Bracker, "Eight Witnesses Balk at Camp Inquiry," *New York Times,* 24 August 1955.

34. Publicity Department, IWO Lodge 5OO, 13 January 1944. Mimeo in IWO Papers, Catherwood Library, Cornell University, Ithaca, NY.

35. Ibid.

36. *Wo-Chi-Ca Yearbook.*

37. Wo-Chi-Ca Reunion list, in the possession of Ann Filardo.

38. "The Wo-Chi-Ca Workshop, A Children's Program of Recreation, Education, and Culture," MS, IWO Papers, n.d. but ca. mid-1940s, Catherwood Library, Cornell University, Ithaca, NY.

39. "Going Wo-Chi-Ca Way," *Wo-Chi-Ca Yearbook.*

40. Ibid.

41. "Paul Robeson Day," *Wo-Chi-Ca Yearbook.*

42 Ibid.

43. *Wo-Chi-Ca Yearbook.*

44. Joe Rabin. "Labor Day 1940," editorial, *Wo-Ki-Mag* (New York: Camp Wo-Chi-Ca, 1940), p. 1 (from the personal collection of Ann Filardo).

45. Dick Crosscup, *The Road to Tomorrow: Wo-Chi-Ca Reunion, February 22, 1945* (New York: Wo-Chi-Ca, 1945), p. 3.

46. Ibid., p. 6.

47. Ibid., p. 9.

48. State of New York, "List of Communist Dominated Camps." Papers of the Joint Legislative Committee on Philanthropic and Charitable Organizations, New York State Library, Albany, and Elsie Suller, personal interview, January 1982.

49. Rex David (*pseud.?*), *Schools and the Crisis,* International Pamphlet #39 (New York: International Publishers, 1934), p. 33, passim.

50. Howard David Langford, *Education and the Social Conflict* (New York: Macmillan, 1936).

51. Zalmen Slesinger, *Education and the Class Struggle: A Critical Examination of the Liberal Educator's Program for Social Reconstruction* (New York: Covici-Friede, 1937).

52. For a more complete discussion of Communist attitudes toward education, see Barry Rubin, "Marxism and Education—Radical Thought and Educational Theory in the 1930s," *Science and Society* 36 (summer 1972).

53. Personal interview, Joan Studer Levine, New York, 27 March 1986.

54. State of New York, *Report of the Joint Legislative Committee on Charitable and Philanthropic Agencies and Organizations* (New York: State of New York, 1956), p. 17.

55. Personal interview, Joan Studer Levine, New York, 27 March 1986.

56. Carleton Mabee, "Margaret Mead and a 'Pilot Experiment' in Progressive and Interracial Education: The Downtown Community School," *New York History* (January 1984): 10, 18.

57. Ibid., passim.

58. Norman Studer "The Story of Camp Woodland,"edited by Joan Studer Levine, songsheet for *The Woodland Sampler*, a tape of songs collected and written at Camp Woodland (New York, 1987), p. 1.

59. *Woodland Brochure* (New York: Camp Woodland, n.d. but ca.1949/1950), p. 1.

60. Ibid.

61. *Neighbors; A Record of Catskills Life*, 1946–1960. From 1941 to 1945 Camp Woodland published yearbooks every summer around different themes and with different titles.

62. A. A. Hartwell, "Exploration: Unearthing Local History and Folklore with the People of the Catskills"—an offprint from *American Heritage* (April 1948), p. 2.

63. Ibid., p. 3.

64. It was not completely unsuccessful because in the 1970s the new library at nearby SUNY–New Paltz was named for Sojourner Truth.

65. Ellen Schrecker, *No Ivory Tower* (New York: Oxford University Press, 1986), p. 258.

66. David K. Dunaway, "Charles Seeger and Carl Sands: The Composer's Collective Years," *Ethnomusicology* (May 1980): 159.

67. Ibid.

68. Hartwell, "Exploration," p. 4.

69. Norman Cazden et al., *Folk Songs of the Catskills* (Albany: State University of New York Press, 1982).

70. Pete Seeger, "Joseito Fernandez and His Song, 'Guantanamera'," *Daily World* (New York), 20 October 1979, p. 12.

71. Neila Miller, "Pete Visits Us," *Neighbors* (1949), n.p.

72. Joan Roelofs (a Woodland camper), personal interview, March 1982, and Mabee, "Margaret Mead," p. 18.

73. State of New York, *Hearings of the Joint Legislative Committee on Charitable and Philanthropic Agencies and Organizations,* 24 August 1955, p. 414.

74. Roelofs, personal interview, March 1982.

75. *Catskill Caller,* 17 July 1949, n.p.

76. Courtney Cazden, "Four Comments," in P. Gilmore and A. A. Glatthorn, eds., *Children In and Out of School* (Washington, DC: Center for Applied Linguistics, 1982), p. 215.

77. In discussion with Courtney Cazden and Joan Studer Levine, this story was told to illustrate the special quality of Woodland's relations with its neighbors, and

the differences between Woodland and camps such as Wo-Chi-Ca and Kinderland. At a Camp Woodland reunion sponsored by the Hudson Valley Study Center at SUNY–New Paltz on 4 October 1997, former Woodland campers shared this story with each other and gathered together to sing this song again.

78. *Wo-Chi-Ca Yearbook,* back cover.

Chapter 6. Primers for Revolution

1. The standard history of radical literature in the United States, Rideout's *The Radical Novel in the United States,* which was first published in 1956 by Harvard University Press, contains no mention at all of radical books for children: Walter B. Rideout, *The Radical Novel in the United States* (New York: Hill & Wang, 1966). Recent studies of radical literature for children in other countries include Joachim Schmidt, "The Issue of Youth Literature and Socialism" (about early twentieth-century Germany); Carlo Pesia and Pino Boero, "Gianni Rodari: An Apprecia-tion" (about contemporary Italy); James Fraser, "Walter Crane and His Socialist Children's Book Illustrations"; and Thomas S. Hansen, "Emil and the Emigrés." The first three of these are in *Phaedrus: An International Annual of Children's Literature Research,* vol. 8 (1981); Hansen's work is in *Phaedrus,* vol. 11 (1985).

2. For example, in Cornelia Miegs et al., *A Critical History of Children's Literature* (New York: Macmillan, 1969), p. 503. Trease is the only radical author mentioned. This work states that the first of his books to be published in the United States was *Cue for Treason* (1940); in fact, International published his *Bows against the Barons* and *Comrades for the Charter* in 1934 and *Call to Arms* in 1935.

3. See this chapter's appendix for a complete bibliography of radical books for children's published in the United States in English. Other authors identified with the Communist movement who wrote books for children and young adults were published by mainstream presses during this period. During the 1950s there was little Red-baiting in the children's book field; left-wing authors experienced much success, particularly with books that had civil rights and antiracist themes (personal correspondence, Alan Wald to the author, 4 June 1993). Such works are not included in this study because they were not directly related to the work of the Communist children's organizations.

4. The Massachusetts investigation into Communist activities in the state included a report about two Young Pioneer reading groups in Quincy, Massachusetts, earlier in the decade. One group was reading Martha Campion's *Who Are the Young Pioneers?* and the other was reading William Montgomery Brown's *Science and History for Boys and Girls.* Massachusetts, House Report #2100 (1938). p. 147.

5. The sources for my compilation of titles of children's books are advertisements in the radical press, the archives of International Publishers, my personal collection, and the personal collection of Ernest Rymer.

6. Martha Campion, ed., *New Pioneer Story Book* (New York: New Pioneer Publishing, 1935), p. i.

7. Benjamin Quarles, *Black Abolitionists* (London: Oxford University Press, 1969), pp. 29, 258*n*.

8. *The Child's Anti-Slavery Book.* (New York: Carleton & Porter, 1859; repub. Miami, Florida: Mnemosyne Publishing, 1969).

9. Kenneth Teitelbaum, *Schooling for "Good Rebels": Socialist Education for Children in the United States, 1900–1920* (Philadelphia: Temple University Press, 1993), p. 149.

10. Ibid., pp. 153, 154.

11. Mark Pittenger, *American Socialists and Evolutionary Thought, 1870–1920* (Madison: University of Wisconsin Press, 1993), passim.

12. Marcy, an editor of the *International Socialist Review,* wrote widely on many topics. A selection of her writings was published in 1988: Frederick C. Giffen, ed., *The Tongue of Angels: The Mary Marcy Reader* (Selinsgrove, PA: Susquehanna University Press, 1988).

13. Caroline Nelson, *Nature Talks on Economics* (Chicago: Charles H. Kerr, 1912), p. i.

14. Ibid., p. 16.

15. Mary E. Marcy, *Stories of the Cave People* (Chicago: Charles H. Kerr, 1917), p. 8.

16. Ibid., p. 7.

17. John Spargo, *Socialist Readings for Children* (New York: Women's National Progressive League, 1909), p. 67.

18. John L. Kyser, "The Deposition of Bishop William Montgomery Brown in New Orleans, 1925," *Louisiana History* 8 (winter 1967): 35.

19. Richard Levins, "A Science of Our Own: Marxism and Nature," *Monthly Review* 38 (July/August 1986), p. 3.

20. William Montgomery Brown., *Science and History for Boys and Girls* (Galion, OH: Bradford-Brown Educational Co., 1932), p. 320.

21. John Spargo, *Socialist Readings for Children* (New York: Women's National Progressive League, 1909), p. 12.

22. Mike Gold, "Review of Fairy Tales for Workers' Children," *Worker's Monthly* 4 (October 1925): 572.

23. Helen Kay, *Battle in the Barnyard* (New York: Workers Library Publishers, 1932), p. 9.

24. For historical accounts of the Gastonia strike see among others Theodore Draper, "Gastonia Revisited" *Social Research* 98 (spring 1971) and Liston Pope, *Millhands and Preachers* (New Haven: Yale University Press, 1942). For a discussion of the National Miners Union, see, Linda Nyden "Black Miners in Western Pennsylvania, 1925–31: The NMU and the UMW," *Science and Society* 41 (spring

1977): 69–107, and Alan Singer, "Communists and Coal Miners: Rank-and-File Organizing in the United Mine Workers of America during the 1920s," *Science and Society* 55 (summer 1991): 132–57.

25. Myra Page (Dorothy Markey) wrote her Ph.D. dissertation on Gastonia prior to the strike and later wrote a novel, *The Gathering Storm* (New York: International Publishers, 1932). Page edited issues of the Young Pioneer magazine about the strike for a period. For details of her life, see Christina L. Baker. *In a Generous Spirit: A First Person Biography of Myra Page* (Urbana: University of Illinois Press, 1996).

26. For historical information about Communist efforts to organize African American sharecroppers in Alabama, see Robin Kelley *Hammer and Hoe: Alabama Communists during the Great Depression* (Chapel Hill: University of North Carolina Press, 1990), passim.

27. Martha Campion, *Who Are the Young Pioneers?* (New York: New Pioneer Publishing, 1934), p. 13.

28. The Nicaraguan issue, which in the 1920s concerned the U.S. intervention in that country, was an important issue for radicals, as it would be again during the 1980s.

29. Until Suzanne Strempek Shea's two recent novels, *Selling the Lite of Heaven* (New York: Washington Square Press, 1994) and *Hoopi Shoopi Donna* (New York: Pocket Books, 1996), *Tree by the Waters* was one of the few, and possibly the only, novel dealing with the Polish-American working-class community of western Massachusetts.

Chapter 7. Conclusion

1. See Joseph Starobin, *American Communism in Crisis, 1943–1957* (Cambridge: Harvard University Press, 1972). Starobin was a correspondent for the *Daily Worker.* He wrote this book after leaving the Communist Party during the 1950s.

2. See Zoltan Deak, ed., *This Noble Flame: A Portrait of a Hungarian Newspaper in America, 1902–1982* (New York: Heritage Press, 1982), passim.

3. Itche Goldberg, personal interview, September 1982, and Robert Snyder, "The Paterson Jewish Folk Chorus: Politics, Ethnicity and Musical Culture," *American Jewish History* 74 (September 1982): 27–44.

4. State of New York, *Report of the Joint Legislative Committee on Charitable and Philanthropic Agencies and Organizations, Communist Indoctrination and Training of Children in Summer Camps* (Albany, NY: Williams Press, 1956), p. 5.

5. Ibid., p. 9.

6. Ibid., p. 29.

7. Gil Green, *Cold War Fugitive* (New York: International Publishers, 1984), p. 76.

8. Albert Kahn, *Vengeance on the Young: The Story of the Smith Act Children*

(New York: The Hour Publishers, 1952). This work republished as a chapter of Albert Kahn, *The Game of Death: Effects of the Cold War on Our Children* (New York: Cameron & Kahn, 1953), pp. 151–167, passim.

9. Minutes of a national meeting, Families of Smith Act Victims, 26–27 June 1951, mimeo, Gerson family files, Brooklyn, NY, quoted in Deborah A. Gerson. " 'Is Family Devotion Now Subversive?': Familialism against McCarthyism," in Joanne Meyerowitz, ed., *Not June Cleaver: Women and Gender in Postwar America, 1945–1960* (Philadelphia: Temple University Press, 1994), p. 160. Gerson, a historian, is the daughter of one of New York Smith Act defendants.

10. Jerry Trauber, personal interview, 15 September 1982.

11. Elaine Tyler May, *Homeward Bound: American Families in the Cold War Era,* (New York: Basic Books, 1988), p. 10.

12. Gerson, "Family Devotion," p. 165. See also Kate Weigand, "The Red Menace, the Feminine Mystique, and the Ohio Un-American Activities Commission: Gender and Anti-Communism in Ohio, 1951–1954," in *Journal of Women's History* 3 (winter 1992): 7093, passim. Weigand shows how Communist women called before the Ohio commission both contested and *accepted* the commission's view on the proper domestic sphere for women.

13. Kate Weigand, "Vanguards of Women's Liberation: The Old Left and the Continuity of the Women's Movement in the United States, 1945–1970s," Ph.D. diss., Ohio State University, 1996, p. 278, particularly chapter 7, passim. Weigand argues that it was the contradiction between the more egalitarian gender values of Communist families and their experience in the New Left of the 1960s that led so-called Red Diaper Daughters into leadership roles in the early Women's Liberation movements of the 1960s and 1970s.

14. See Lawrence S. Wittner, *Rebels against War: The American Peace Movement 1933–1983* (Philadelphia: Temple University Press, 1984), chapter 10 and the epilogue.

15. "Red Diaper Babies Grow Up," *Young Guard,* (September 1965): 11.

16. Clayborne Carson, *Struggle: SNCC and the Black Awakening of the 1960s* (Cambridge: Harvard University Press, 1981), p. 162.

17. Marc Eliot, *Death of a Rebel, Starring Phil Ochs and a Small Circle of Friends* (Garden City, NY: Anchor Press/Doubleday, 1979), p. 29.

18. Kirkpatrick Sale, *SDS,* (New York: Random House, 1973), p. 206.

19. James P. O'Brien, "The Development of a New Left in the United States, 1960–1965," Ph.D. diss., University of Wisconsin, 1971, p. 23, quoted in Robert and Michael Meeropol, *We Are Your Sons: The Legacy of Ethel and Julius Rosenberg* (Boston: Houghton Mifflin, 1975), p. 395.

bibliography and sources

Manuscript Collections

Colon, Jesus. Papers. Center for Puerto Rican Studies, Hunter College, New York.

International Publishers. Archives. New York, NY.

IWO papers. Catherwood Library, Cornell University.

New York State Investigations of Radicalism. Papers, 1919, 1930, 1956. New York State Library, Albany, NY.

Reference Center for Marxist Studies. New York, NY.

Studer, Norman. Papers. English Department, State University of New York at New Paltz.

Tamiment Library, New York University.

Primary Sources

Asher, Martha Stone. "Recollections of the Passaic Textile Strike of 1926." Labor's Heritage (April 1990).

Bebel, August. *Woman under Socialism* . Introduction by Lewis Coser. New York: Schocken Books, 1971.

Bedacht, Max. *Labor Fraternalism: The Fraternal Principals and Program of the IWO*. New York: National Education Department, International Workers Order, 1941.

Bedacht, Max. *The Organizer and His Problems: A Manual for Builders of the IWO*. New York: International Workers Order, n.d., ca. 1935.

———. "Report of the General Secretary to the Fourth National Convention of the IWO." Pittsburgh: IWO, 1938.

Benson, Allan L. *Socialism Made Plain*. Milwaukee, WI: Milwaukee Social-Democratic Publishing, 1904.

Bloor, Ella Reeve. *We Are Many*. New York: International Publishers, 1940.

Calhoun, Arthur W. *A Social History of the American Family from Colonial Times to the Present,* Vol. 3: *Since the Civil War.* Cleveland, OH: Arthur Clark, 1919.

David, Rex. *Schools and the Crisis.* International Pamphlets No. 39. New York: International Publishers and Labor Research Association, 1934.

Dillings, Elizabeth. *The Red Network.* Kenilworth, IL: published by the author, 1934; reprint edition, New York: Arno Press, 1977.

Dushkin, Alexander. *Survey of Jewish Education in Los Angeles, California, with special Reference to the Bureau of Jewish Education and Its Affiliated Schools.* Mimeo. New York: Bureau of Jewish Education, 1944.

Eisman, Harry. *An American Boy In the Soviet Union.* New York: Youth Publishers, 1934.

Gilfillan, Lauren (Harriet Woodbridge Gilfillan, *pseud.*). *I Went to Pit College.* New York: Viking, 1934.

Gold, Mike. "A Little Bit of Millennium." In Michael Folsom, ed. *Mike Gold: A Literary Anthology.* New York: International Publishers, 1972.

———. *Change the World.* New York: International Publishers, 1935.

Goldstein, David. *Socialism: A Nation of Fatherless Children.* Edited by Martha Moore Avery. Boston: Union News League, 1903.

Hillquit, Morris, and Father John Ryan. *Socialism: Promise or Menace.* New York: Macmillan, 1914.

Hoernle, Edwin. *Manual for Leaders of Children's Groups.* Berlin: Young Communist International, n.d., ca. 1924.

Hutchins, Grace. *Children under Capitalism* . New York: International Publishers, 1933.

International Workers Order. *Five Years of the International Workers Order, 1930–1935.* New York: National Executive Committee of the IWO, 1935.

International Workers Order, junior section. *Proceedings of National Conference: Labor's Children in a World at War.* New York City, October 25–26, 1941.

Kahn, Albert. *The Game of Death: The Effects of the Cold War on Our Children.* New York: Cameron & Kahn, 1953.

Kinderland. *Book of the 1st Camp Kinderland Reunion.* New York: Camp Kinderland, 1979.

Kingsbury, Mary. *Socialism as an Educative and Social Force on the East Side.* Boston: Christian Social Union, 1898.

Langford, Howard David. *Education and the Social Conflict.* Kappa Delta Pi Research Publications. New York: Macmillan, 1936.

Liber, Benzion. *The Child and the Home: Essays in the Rational Bringing-up of Children.* 1st. edition, 1922. New York: Vanguard, 1927.

Matthews, J. B. "The Commies Go After the Kids." *American Legion Magazine* 47 (December 1949): 14–15.

Michelfelder, William F. "Adolescent Reds." *Commonweal* 23 (24 January 1936): 357.

Ocken, Sophia. "A Mother and Child Unit." *Party Organizer* 10 (July 1937): 35–37.

Party Organizer. "Our New Children's Magazine." *Party Organizer*. 4 (May 1931): 16–17.

Paul, Eden, and Cedar Eden. *Prolecult* (Proletarian Culture). New York: Thomas Seltzer, 1921.

Resnick, Sid. "Recalling My Shule Days." *Jewish Currents* 29 (January 1975).

Sailer, Agnes. "Miners' Children at Play" *Progressive Education* 9 (November 1932): 507–8.

Segal, Edith. *Victory Verses for Young Americans.* New York: IWO, n.d., ca. 1942.

Slesinger, Zalmen. *Education and the Class Struggle: A Critical Examination of the Liberal Educator's Program for Social Reconstruction*. New York: Civici-Friede, 1937.

"Socialist Sunday Schools and Morality." *Literary Digest* 12 (1895): 174.

Solidarity [Official Organ of the Workers International Relief, American Section] 1. (August 1929).

"Some Socialist and Anarchist Views of Education." *Educational Review* 17 (January 1898): 1–16.

Spargo, John. *Applied Socialism: A Study of the Applications of Socialist Principals to the State*. New York: B. W. Huebsch, 1912.

———. *Socialism and Motherhood*. New York: B. W. Huebsch, 1914.

———. *Socialist Readings for Children.* New York: Women's National Progressive League, 1909.

Trauber, Jerry. "Report on the Junior Section to the Fourth National Convention of the IWO." Pittsburgh: IWO, 1938.

———. "Report to the Fifth National Convention of the IWO, 3rd National Junior Conference." June 1940.

Vorse. Mary Heaton. *The Passaic Textile Strike, 1926–1927.* Passaic, NJ: General Relief Committee of Textile Strikers, 1927.

Whitney, R. M. *Reds in America*. New York: Beckwith Press, 1924.

Winston, Henry. *Building Character and Education in the Spirit of Socialism.* New York: New Age, 1939.

Worker's Child 1 (January 1934).

Workers Life (organ of the WIR) (June 1932).

Young Americans for Freedom. "Red Diaper Babies." *New Guard* (September 1965) 6–12.

Young Communist International, Executive Committee. *The Child of the Worker: A Collection of Facts and the Remedy*. Berlin-Schweneberg: Publishing House of the Young International, 1923.

Young Communist League. "The Road to Mass Organization of Proletarian Children: Decisions of the Fourth International Conference of Leaders of Communist Children's Leagues, Moscow, September, 1929." New York:

Young Communist League/Youth International Publishers, 1930.

———. *Stand Ready: The Call of the First International Children's Congress to All Proletarian Children*. London: Young Communist League, 1929.

———. *Towards a Mass Young Communist League*. New York: Young Communist League, 1933.

Young Workers (Communist) League of America. MS. *Bulletin on the Reorganization of Pioneer Groups*. November 1925.

Government Documents

Massachusetts, Commonwealth of. House. *Special Commission to Investigate Activities within Massachusetts of Communistic, Fascist, Nazi and other Subversive Organizations*. House report no. 2100 1938.U.S. Congress. House. Committee on Un-American Activities. *Guide to Subversive Organizations and Publications (and Appendix)* revised, May 14, 1951

New York, State of. *State Report of the Joint Legislative Committee on Charitable and Philanthropic Agencies and Organizations*. New York Legislative Document #62 (1956).

———. Insurance Department. *Report on the Examination of the International Workers Order, Inc.,* Mimeo. New York (1950).

———. *Minutes of the Proceedings of the Joint Legislative Committee on Charitable and Philanthropic Agencies and Organizations*. Leg. 074.8–2, August 23, 1955.

U.S. Congress. House. Special Committee to Investigate Communist Activities. *Investigation of Communist Propaganda*. 71st Congress. 2nd Session, 1930.

U.S. Supreme Court. *Stromberg vs. California*. 283 U.S. 359 (1931). [Case concerning the constitutionality of a California law banning the public showing of the Red Flag. The case was brought initially against a Communist children's camp near Los Angeles *(People vs. Mintz.* 106 Cal. App. 725 290 Pac 93 [1930]).]

Secondary Sources

Avrich, Paul. *The Modern School Movement*. Princeton, NJ: Princeton University Press, 1980.

Ahola, David John. *Finnish-Americans and International Communism: A Study of Finnish American Communism from Bolshevization to the Demise of the Third International*. Lanham, MD: University Press of America, 1982.

Beck, John. "Highlander's Junior Union Camps, 1940–1944: Workers' Children and Working-Class Culture," *Labor's Heritage*, vol. 5 (spring 1993).

———. "With the Children of the Working Class Lies the Future of America: The Pioneer Youth of America." Unpublished paper.

Bell, Daniel. *Marxian Socialism in the United States*. Princeton, NJ: Princeton University Press, 1967.

Billington, James H. *Fire in the Minds of Men*. New York: Basic Books, 1980.

Blackmar, Betsy. "Going to the Mountains: A Social History." In Betsy Blackmar et al., *Resorts of the Catskills*. New York: St.Martin's, 1979.

Buhle, Mari Jo. *Women and American Socialism, 1870–1920*. Urbana: University of Illinois Press, 1981.

Cantwell, Robert. *When We Were Good: The Folk Revival*. Cambridge, MA: Harvard University Press, 1996.

Chernin, Kim. *In My Mother's House*. New Haven: Ticknor & Fields, 1983.

Cohn, Norman. *The Pursuit of the Millennium*. New York: Oxford University Press, 1970.

Cobb, William. "From Utopian Isolation to Radical Activism: Commonwealth College, 1925–1935." *Arkansas Historical Quarterly* 32 (summer 1973).

Cornell, Richard. "The Origins and Development of the Communist Youth International, 1914–1924." Ph.D. diss., Columbia University, 1965.

Deak, Zoltan. *This Noble Flame: Portrait of a Hungarian Newspaper in America, 1902–1982*. New York: Heritage, 1982.

Denisoff, Serge. *Songs of Protest, War and Peace: A Bibliography and Discography*. Santa Barbara, CA: ABC-Clio, 1973.

Denning, Michael. *The Cultural Front*. London: Verso, 1996.

Dennis, Peggy. *Autobiography of an American Communist*. Westport, CT: Lawrence Hill, 1977.

Ditzion, Sidney. *Marriage, Morals and Sex in America: A History of Ideas*. New York: Bookman, 1953.

Dixler, Elsa Jane. "The Woman Question: Women in the Communist Party, 1929–41." Ph.D. diss., Yale University, 1974.

Draper, Theodore. *The Roots of American Communism*. New York: Viking, 1957.

———. *American Communism and Soviet Russia*. New York: Viking, 1960.

———. "Gastonia Revisited." *Social Research* 38 (spring 1971).

Duberman, Martin. *The Anti-Slavery Vanguard*. Princeton, NJ: Princeton University Press, 1965.

Dunaway, David K. "Charles Seeger and Carl Sands: The Composer's Collective Years." *Ethnomusicology* (May 1980).

Egerton, John. "Visions of Utopia." *Southern Exposure* (March, 1979): 38–47.

Eppe, Heinrich. *Seventy Years of the Socialistic Youth International: A History of the International Organizations of Children and Juveniles*. Bonn: SIE, 1977.

Epstein, Melech. *The Jew and Communism*. New York: Trade Union Sponsoring Committee, 1959.

Gartner, Lloyd D., ed. *Jewish Education in the United States: A Documentary History*. New York: Teacher's College Press, 1969.

Georgianna, Daniel, and Roberta H. Aaronson. *The Strike of '28*. New Bedford, MA: Spinner Publications, 1993.

Gerson, Deborah A. " 'Is Family Devotion Now Subversive?' Familialism against McCarthyism." In Joanne Meyerowitz, ed. *Not June Cleaver: Women and Gender in Postwar America, 1945–1960.* Philadelphia, PA: Temple University Press, 1994.

Graham, Patricia. *Progressive Education: From Arcady to Academe, the Progressive Education Association, 1919–1955.* New York: Teachers College Press, 1967.

Green, Archie. *Only a Miner.* Urbana: University of Illinois Press, 1972.

Green, Gil. *Cold War Fugitive.* New York: International Publishers, 1984.

Green, James. *Grass-roots Socialism.* Baton Rouge: Louisiana University Press, 1978.

Goodwyn, Laurence. *The Populist Moment.* New York: Oxford University Press, 1978.

Gornick, Vivian. *The Romance of American Communism.* New York: Basic Books, 1977.

Hartwell, A. A. "Exploration: Unearthing Local History and Folklore with the People of the Catskills." Offprint from *American Heritage* (April, 1948).

Hasome, Marius. *World Worker's Educational Movements: Their Social Significance.* New York: Columbia University Press, 1931.

Hine, Robert. *California Utopian Communities.* Berkeley: University of California Press, 1983.

Horn, Max. "The Intercollegiate Socialist Society, 1905–1921: Origins of the Modern American Student Movement." Ph.D. diss., Columbia University, 1975.

Hoglund, A. William. *Finnish Immigrants in America.* Madison: University of Wisconsin Press, 1960.

Howe, Daniel Walker. *The Political Culture of the American Whigs.* Chicago: University of Chicago Press, 1979.

Howe, Irving. *The World of Our Fathers.* New York: Harcourt, Brace & Jovanovich, 1976.

———, and Lewis Coser. *The American Communist Party: A Critical History.* New York: Frederick Praeger, 1962.

Howkins, Alun. "Class against Class: The Communist Party of Great Britain, 1930–1935." In Frank Gloversmith, *Class, Culture and Social Change.* Atlantic Highlands, NJ: Humanities Press, 1980.

Hummasti, Paul. *Finnish Radicals in Astoria, Oregon, 1904–1940: A Study of Immigrant Socialism.* New York: Arno, 1979.

Hurwitz, Maximillian. *The Workmen's Circle: Its History, Ideals, Organization and Institutions.* New York: Workmen's Circle, 1936.

Isserman, Maurice. *Which Side Were You On?: The American Communist Party during the Second World War.* Middletown, CT: Wesleyan University Press, 1982.

Hobsbawm, E. J. *Primitive Rebels: Studies in Archaic Forms of Social Movement in the 19th and 20th Centuries.* New York: W. W. Norton, 1965.

Karni, Michael. "Yhteishyua—or for the Common Good: Finnish Radicalism in the Western Great Lakes Region, 1900–1940." Ph.D. diss., University of Minnesota, 1975.

Keeran, Roger. *The Communist Party and the Auto Workers Unions.* Bloomington: Indiana University Press, 1980.

Keeran, Roger. "National Groups and the Popular Front: The Case of the International Workers Order." *Journal of American Ethnic History* 14 (spring 1995).

Kertzer, David I. *Comrades and Christians: Religion and Political Struggle in Communist Italy.* Cambridge: Cambridge University Press, 1980.

Kivisto, Peter. *Immigrant Socialists in the United States: The Case of the Finns and the Left.* Cranbury, NJ; Farleigh-Dickenson University Press, 1984.

Klehr, Harvey. *Communist Cadre.* Stanford, CA: Hoover Institution Press, 1978.

———. *The Heyday of American Communism: The Depression Decade.* New York: Basic Books, 1984.

Kolehmainen, John I. *A History of the Finns in Ohio, Western Pennsylvania, and West Virginia.* Ohio: Ohio Finnish-American Historical Society, 1977.

———. *The Finns in America: A Bibliographical Guide to Their History.* Hancock, MI: Finnish-American Historical Library, Suomi College, 1947.

Koch, Raymond, and Charlotte Koch. *Educational Commune: The Story of Commonwealth College.* New York: Schocken Books, 1972.

Kostiainen, Auvo. *The Forging of Finnish-American Communism, 1917–1924: A Study of Ethnic Radicalism.* Turko, Finland: Turun Yliopisto, 1978.

———. "For or against Americanization? The Case of the Finnish Immigrant Radicals." In Dirk Hoerder, ed., *American Labor and Immigration History, 1877–1920s: Recent European Research.* Urbana: University of Illinois Press, 1983.

Kraditor, Aileen S. *The Radical Persuasion, 1890–1917: Aspects of the Intellectual History and the Historiography of Three American Radical Organizations.* Baton Rouge: Louisiana University Press, 1981.

Kyser, John L. "The Deposition of Bishop William Montgomery Brown in New Orleans, 1925." *Louisiana History* 8 (winter 1967).

Lasky, Melvin. *Utopia and Revolution .* Chicago: University of Chicago Press, 1976.

Lazare, Jane. *On Loving Men.* New York: Dial, 1978.

Leslie, W. B. "Coming of Age in Urban America: The Socialist Alternative, 1901–1920." *Teacher's College Record* 85 (spring 1984): 459–76.

Lidtke, Vernon. *Alternative Culture: Socialist Labor in Imperial Germany.* New York: Oxford University Press, 1985.

Liebman, Arthur. *Jews and the Left.* New York: John Wiley, 1979.

Lieberman, Robbie. "People's Songs: American Communism and the Politics of

Culture." *Radical History Review* 36 (fall 1986).

Lynd, Robert, and Helen Lynd. *Middletown: A Study in Modern American Culture*. San Diego: Harcourt, Brace & Jovanovich, 1929.

Mabee, Carleton. "Margaret Mead and a 'Pilot Experiment' in Progressive and Interracial Education: The Downtown Community School." *New York History* (January 1984).

MacIntyre, Stuart. *Little Moscows: Communism and Working-Class Militancy in Inter-War Britain*. London: Croom-Helm, 1980.

Macleod, David. *Building Character in the American Boy: Boy Scouts, YMCA and Their Forerunners, 1870–1920*. Madison: University of Wisconsin Press, 1983.

Marsh, Margaret S. *Anarchist Women, 1870–1920*. Philadelphia, PA: Temple University Press, 1981.

Mark, Arthur. "Two Libertarian Educators: Elizabeth Byrn Ferm and Alexis Constantine Ferm (1857–1971)." Ph.D. diss., Columbia Teacher's College, 1973.

May, Elaine Tyler. *Homeward Bound: American Families in the Cold War*. New York: Basic Books, 1988.

Meeropol, Robert, and Michael Meeropol. *We Are Your Sons: The Legacy of Ethel and Julius Rosenberg*. Boston: Houghton-Mifflin, 1975.

Naison, Mark. *Communists in Harlem during the Depression*. Urbana: University of Illinois Press, 1983.

———. "Lefties and Righties: The Communist Party and Sports during the Great Depression." In Donald Spivey, ed., *Sports in America*. Westport, CT: Greenwood Press, 1985.

Nelson, Steve, James Barrett, and Rob Buck. *Steve Nelson: American Radical*. Pittsburgh, PA: University of Pittsburgh Press, 1981.

Noonan, Kathryn. "Proletarian Fraternalism and the Junior Section of the International Workers' Order." Unpublished undergraduate paper, Cornell University, August 1980.

Nyden, Linda. "Black Miners in Western Pennsylvania, 1925–1931: The NMU and the UMW." *Science and Society*.41 (spring 1977): 69–101.

James P. O'Brien, "The Development of a New Left in the United States, 1960–1965." Ph.D. diss., University of Wisconsin, 1971.

Parker, Sandra. "An Educational Assessment of the Yiddish Secular School Movements in the United States." In Joshua Fishman, *Never Say Die! A Thousand Years of Yiddish in Jewish Life and Letters*. The Hague: Mouton Publishers, 1977.

Peterson, Patti McGill. "The Young Socialist Movement in the America from 1905–1940: A Study of the Young People's Socialist League." Ph.D. diss., University of Wisconsin, 1974.

Pittenger, Mark. *American Socialists and Evolutionary Thought, 1870–1920*.

Madison: University of Wisconsin Press, 1993.

Prynn, David. "The Woodcraft Folk and the Labour Movement, 1925–1970." *Journal of Contemporary History* 18 (1983): 79–95.

Reese, William. "Partisans of the Proletariat: The Socialist Working-Class and the Milwaukee Schools, 1890–1912." *History of Education Quarterly.* 21 (fall 1981): 3–50.

Reid, F. "Socialist Sunday Schools in Britain, 1892–1939." *International Review of Social History* 40 (1966).

Robinson, Lori, and Bill De Yong. "Socialism in the Sunshine: The Roots of Ruskin, Florida." *Tampa Bay History* (spring/summer 1982).

Roth, Guenther. *The Social Democrats in Imperial Germany* . Totowa, NJ: Bedminster Press, 1963.

Rubin, Barry. "Marxism and Education—Radical Thought and Educational Theory in the 1930s." *Science and Society* 36 (summer 1972).

Saroff, Sophie, and Arthur Tobier. *Stealing the State, Sophie Saroff: An Oral History.* New York: Community Documentation Workshop, 1983.

Schrecker, Ellen. *No Ivory Tower.* New York: Oxford University Press, 1986.

Seeger, Pete. *The Incompleat Folksinger.* New York: Simon & Schuster, 1972.

Shapiro, Judah J. *The Friendly Society: A History of the Workmen's Circle.* New York: Media Judaica, 1970.

Snyder, Robert. "The Paterson Jewish Folk Chorus: Politics, Ethnicity and Musical Culture." *American Jewish History* 74 (September 1984).

Sokolova, E. S., V. V. Lebedenskii, and V. A. Pushkina. "Children's Democratic Organizations." *Great Soviet Encyclopedia,* vol. 18. New York: Macmillan, 1975.

Studer, Norman, Norman Cazden, and Herbert Haufrecht. *Folksongs of the Catskills.* Albany, NY. State University of New York Press, 1982.

Tager, Florence. "Radical Theory and Practice in Education, 1900–1920." Ph.D. diss., Ohio State University, 1978.

Teitelbaum, Kenneth. *Schooling For "Good Rebels": Socialist Education for Children in the United States, 1900–1920.* Philadelphia, PA: Temple University Press, 1993.

———, and William Reese. "American Socialist Pedagogy and Experimentation in the Progressive Era: The Socialist Sunday School." *History of Education Quarterly* 23 (winter 1983).

Tien, Jocelyn. "Educational Theories of American Socialists, 1900–1920." Ph.D. diss., Michigan State University, 1973.

Trillin, Calvin. "U.S. Journal: The Bronx." *New Yorker* (1 August 1977).

Työmies Society. *For the Common Good: Finnish Immigrants and the Radical Response to Industrial America.* Superior, Wisconsin: Työmies Society, 1977.

Weigand, Kate. "The Red Menace, the Feminine Mystique, and the Ohio Un-American Activities Commission: Gender and Anti-Communism in Ohio, 1951–1954." *Journal of Women's History* 3 (winter 1992).

————. "Vanguards of Women's Liberation: The Old Left and the Continuity of the Women's Movement in the United States, 1945–1970s." Ph.D. diss., Ohio State University, 1996.

Williams, James Mickel. *Human Aspects of Unemployment and Relief.* Chapel Hill: University of North Carolina Press, 1933.

Worsley, Peter. *The Trumpet Shall Sound.* London: MacGibbon & Kee, 1957.

Personal Interviews by the Author

Antonsen, Erdine (writer on the family for the *Daily Worker,* in the 1940s), spring 1982.

Beck, Eda (Harry Eisman's sister and a former Young Pioneer), fall 1983.

Ann Filardo, 15 August 1993.

Gerson, Sophie (a former Young Pioneer activist and leader), February 1984.

Goldberg, Itche (educational director of the IWO and director of the Shules), fall 1983.

Kirschner, Ethel (Nature Friends), November 1986.

Levine, Joan Studer (daughter of Norman Studer, director of Camp Woodland), 27 March 1986.

Pevsner, Sam (youth director of the IWO), January 1982.

Roelofs, Joan (former Woodland camper), January 1982.

Rymer, Ernest (national director of the Young Pioneers, 1928–1934, and of the junior section, IWO, in the early 1940s), January and September 1982.

Segal, Edith (dance teacher at Kinderland), January 1982.

Suller, Elsie (longtime Kinderland staff member and director of the camp during the 1960s and 1970s), fall 1981.

Trauber, Jerry (national director, junior section, IWO, 1930–1939), 15 September 1982.

index